# The Sketches Of Life

I0569510

John NT

# The Sketches Of Life

Presented by:   Ly Cam Ha
Illustration:   Dz & Hannah
Cover artists:  Tomy
Published by:   WuWei Press
California, USA

ISBN:  979-8-9878147-3-4

PART I
**COGITATION**
17


PART II
**AUTUMN HAS COME**
65


PART III
**REALM OF HUMANS**
169

# TABLE OF CONTENTS

**PART I: COGITATION** 17

1. Talking to Myself 18

2. The Strangest Thing About Life 19

3. What is Meditation? 20

4. The Way to the Buddha 22

5. Prayers to the Buddha 25

6. First Days in a Foreign Land 26

7. Goodbye, Sorrow! 30

8. Roses and Thorns 33

9. Let Me Go Home! 34

10. Human Beings and Perfection 36

11. The Equation of Life 40

12. Admonishing Ourselves, Admonishing Others 43

13. Where Are You, My Country's Spirit? 46

14. Who Are We, My Country? 50

15. Which Speck of Dust Was Turned Into My Body... 54

16. The Fansipan Journey 60

**PART II: AUTUMN HAS COME** 65

1. Humanity, Then and Now 66

2. Reflections of Life 67

3. Navigating Life's Waves 69

4. Boredom of Attachment 71

5. Time of Dust 73

6. Arrogance and Envy 74

7. The Hard Truth 76

8. Lessons in Letting Go 77

9. Legacy and Freedom 78

10. Dedication and Order 80

11. Carefree Friendship 81

12. A Free Soul 83

13. Emotional Love ... 84

14. The Wisdom Puzzle ... 85

15. Wise or Foolish, Be Alive in the Now ... 86

16. Graceless and Innocent ... 87

17. Patient Means Proactive ... 88

18. You Need Your Enemy ... 89

19. Thank You ... 90

20. The Power of Discretion ... 91

21. Wisdom and the Teacher ... 92

22. Love Yourself - Love the Nation ... 93

23. Knowledge and Wisdom ... 95

24. Painful Indifference ... 97

25. Life's Little Ironies ... 99

26. Conscience Is the Highest Court ... 100

27. Live in the Now ... 101

28. Count on Yourself ... 102

29. Reading Is a Duty ... 103

30. Life's Crossroads ... 104

31. Predestined Fate ... 105

32. Respecting Ourselves ... 106

33. Never See the Betrayer Again ... 107

34. Observing the Precepts ... 108

35. Lonely Traveler ... 109

36. The Tug of Dreams and Resistance ... 110

37. The Real Pursuit ... 112

38. Human Life ... 114

39. The Push and Pull of Life ... 115

40. The Meaning of Life ... 117

41. Property Is a Burden ... 118

42. Living Fully, One Small Step at a Time ... 119

43. Points of View and Personality ... 120

44. Hard-to-Explain Stuff ... 121

| | |
|---|---|
| 45. Body and Mind | 122 |
| 46. Faith and the Eternal Universe | 124 |
| 47. Take Your Step | 126 |
| 48. If Tomorrow Never Came | 127 |
| 49. Lust | 128 |
| 50. Indifference and Curiosity | 129 |
| 51. Gloomy Day | 130 |
| 52. Restive Passion | 131 |
| 53. Hanging Out with Friends | 132 |
| 54. The Bragger | 133 |
| 55. Two Sides of the Same Coin | 134 |
| 56. Experience and Tranquility | 136 |
| 57. Useful Illness | 137 |
| 58. Loneliness as a Delight | 138 |
| 59. Indifferent Beauty | 139 |
| 60. The Confidence of Arrogance | 140 |
| 61. Agreement with Nature | 141 |
| 62. Forbidden Things Are Always Tempting | 142 |
| 63. The Laws of Life | 143 |
| 64. Wishes and Moments | 144 |
| 65. Don't Be a Pathetic Infantile Guy | 145 |
| 66. Observe Your Self-Adjusted Precepts | 146 |
| 67. Your Own Festival | 148 |
| 68. Stripping It Down | 149 |
| 69. Courage and Responsibility | 150 |
| 70. Temporary Happiness | 151 |
| 71. Making Love Is an Art Form | 152 |
| 72. Unlucky | 153 |
| 73. Mountain Tops and Forests | 154 |
| 74. Always Be Ready | 155 |
| 75. Delicate and Profound | 156 |
| 76. Fragile Emotions | 157 |

77. Health ... 158

78. Knowledge Is Not Enough ... 159

79. The Path from Misery to Happiness ... 160

80. Misperceptions ... 162

81. Why the Rush? ... 163

82. A Look at Myself ... 164

83. Life Desires ... 165

84. Just Give and Forget It ... 166

**Part III: REALM OF HUMANS** ... 169

1. The Journey of Life ... 171

2. Morality ... 172

3. Nirvana and Hell ... 173

4. Body ... 174

5. Politeness ... 175

6. Pleasure and Pain ... 176

7. Sins ... 178

8. Mind ... 179

9. The Price of Greatness ... 181

10. Choice ... 182

11. Letting Go and Waiting ... 183

12. Nation and People ... 184

13. Humans ... 185

14. Drivers ... 186

15. Security Guards ... 187

16. Sense of humor ... 188

17. Dedication ... 189

18. Women ... 190

19. Men ... 191

20. Love ... 192

21. Music ... 193

22. Regret ... 194

23. The Art of Stillness — 195
24. Marks of Perfection — 196
25. Drunk — 198
26. Whispers and Rumors — 200
27. Origin — 202
28. Hatred — 203
29. Childhood Performance — 204
30. Sweethearts — 205
31. Seeing a Doctor Means Comfort — 206
32. Never See Old Memories Again — 207
33. Solitary as a Reminder — 208
34. Haircut Day — 209
35. Liar — 210
36. Jail — 211
37. The Swing of Life — 212
38. Lost in the Echoes — 213
39. Decent Figure — 214
40. Going to the Restroom — 215
41. Exile and the Scent of Home — 216
42. Home garden (I) — 218
43. Home Garden (II) — 219
44. Provocation — 220
45. Sport — 221
46. Ideal of Life — 222
47. A Good Layperson — 223
48. Our Religions — 225
49. What Women Want — 226
50. Weird guy — 227
51. Plant styling — 228
52. Whispers of Autumn — 230
53. New architecture — 232
54. Joy of Life — 233

55. Private Shelter — 234
56. Mother and Lessons — 235
57. Sound of Time — 236
58. Goodbye Old Year — 237
59. Lost — 239
60. Book of My Life — 240
61. Vegetarian Diet — 241
62. Wind of Change — 243
63. Lustful Guys — 244
64. Work — 245
65. Wine — 246
66. Memory — 248
67. Mistakes and Regrets — 250
68. Attached — 252
69. Teacher — 253
70. Words of Love (I) — 255
71. Words of Love (II) — 257
72. Words of Love (III) — 258
73. Drunk Mosquito — 259
74. God — 260
75. Flower Fragrance — 261
76. Trap — 262
77. The Art of Cooking — 263
78. Keep Silent — 265

## Some Words for Sketches of Life

*"Take advantage of the human boat, free yourself from sorrow's mighty stream."*

Shantideva

The Way of the Bodhisattva

Since its earliest inception as a literary form in ancient Chinese, Vietnamese, Roman and Greek literature, the nonfiction memoir has undergone at least a thousand years of development and change. The form exists in such an inclusive variety that it would be impossible for me to share them all with you without using up too much of the space I want to use for saying other things, but consider this range: from Seneca's wise adages, all the way to post-apocalyptic illustrated novels. In English the expressions of the memoir have taken many different forms, from fairly straight-forward narratives told from the first- person point of view about a wide variety of experiences and subjects, to wildly experimental writing that begs to exist on a literal as well as on a metaphorical plane, simultaneously. The variety of these forms has also been available to the Vietnamese writer, at least since the French War, and Vietnamese literary history is marked with such notable works of nonfiction as Nguyen Du's The Tale of Kieu, and more recently Bao Ninh's The Sorrow of War. And although the former is considered most widely an epic poem, and the latter an autobiographical novel, they both exist in the realm of nonfiction and memoir because of their reliance on real events and real people, but not on standard literary forms. Particularly important to the development of style in John NT's writing has been nonfiction works by Hai Thuong Lan Ong (Thuong Kinh Ky Su), Trinh Cong Son (Toi La Ai), and Vo Nguyen Giap's famous memoir, Tong Tap Hoi Ky.

The memoir is the most personal of all the nonfiction forms. And although memoir writing needs to be rooted in real experience, it is not held to the same rigorous standards of fact-checking as autobiography or biography. Memoir allows a bending of the narrative to suit the particular writer's goals.

There's an old Chinese story about a detective who is called to the scene of a murder in Beijing that took place in a crowded marketplace. When he's finished interviewing the witnesses he returns to his office and realizes that he has one hundred different versions of the same crime. At first he's confused, and wonders which one is the right one, but then it occurs to him that the right one, the most accurate one, was the one that included everyone's version of events. This is what I mean about the flexibility of the genre. The story of the crime could be told from any one of the hundred witnesses, and in his book, John NT takes full advantage of nonfiction's generous literary opportunities.

Part Henry Miller and part Thich Nhat Hanh, John NT has discovered a fresh way to look at the difficulties of living faithfully in a faithless world. He achieves this through his reliance on the kind of honesty that only the most interesting writing brings to us. This is the honesty of belief, and not simply revelations of the literal world. It's an honesty that allows the writer to open his life in the most intimate and self-revealing ways. But although it is a dharmic journey that John NT undertakes and narrates here, what is revealed is not the Buddha, but a lover of the dharma, and of beautiful women, good cigars, and fine wine. He never hesitates to confront even the most confounding aspects of our nature with the Buddha's teaching and the result is a rich, interesting and engaging narrative of one man's journey to find his way.

Notably, there is a distinct absence of ego throughout these autobiographical tales that are driven instead by a fierce truth-telling, and by the author's embrace of a point of view that insistsa we must tell the truth, no matter what it may say about who we are and what we believe. His pedagogical method is clear. Initially he encourages us to think about the advantages and excellence of our goals, and then we are to learn through meditation about the consequences of being weak or backsliding. It sounds almost too easy to say.

John NT's wise and rough-hewn Buddhist principles shine a light on the most challenging facets of our daily lives and suggest, not too unlike the Taoist vision, that the full development of one's character can only come from the cultivation of the inner self. In turn, this kind of self-knowledge comes only from the awe of devotion to a spiritual life. John NT deeply understands the way of the Dharma, but he translates that knowledge into a diction that is rich, humorous and illuminated by his ironically grounded humanness, so it is therefore accessible to a wide range of readers.

Because of John NT's ability to discuss deeply felt spiritual ideas in the clearest possible language, these lessons do not feel as if they've come from on high. But what gives them their power is that they have all been lived most fully by the author. Lived and then presented to us in their nuanced form without any adornment. The teaching present in this book is not simply theoretical, although the theory is there if you look closely enough, but it is more a practical guide to living a compassionate life and the great rewards of such a life.

John NT never tells us that this is an easy path, but his engaging book convinces us that it is a possible one, waiting for us all at the end of a compassionate life.

John NT was born in 1966 in Ha Noi to school teacher parents. Growing up in a family who practiced ancestor worship and who visited the temple on a regular basis, he nevertheless temporarily abandoned such study and devoted himself to the life of an international businessman. Trained in theoretical physics and mathematics, his successful business career, which began at Vietnam's National Atomic Energy Institute, allowed him the opportunity to enjoy all of life's pleasures. But he grew weary of this life and turned instead to meditation and study. He has published two books on Vietnamese cultural issues, two about management techniques, and two about economic issues. This book was written as he approached his fiftieth year out of his desire to take the Buddha's teaching out of the temple and the meditation center, and bring it directly to the people, a long-held tenet of Mahayana Buddhism.

*Bruce Weigl,*
*October, 2022, Oberlin, Ohio*

# PART I
# COGITATION

# 1. TALKING TO MYSELF

It's no secret that smiling is often better than agonizing. A smile, they say, can be the best remedy, no matter the problem. Some women even say, *"Your smile melted my heart."* Yet, finding the time for a genuine smile can feel elusive. Life, it seems, is filled with worries. So how do we find comfort? Perhaps by letting go of what is forgettable, loosening our grip on winning and losing, and simply embracing the present. If only we could laugh more freely—maybe then life would be a bit more fun.

Life has its twists and turns, its empty lanes and deserts. It constantly presents us with choices, some as heavy as promises, others as light as a passing thought. Each decision comes with its own cost, to be paid either upfront or later down the road. We can't expect to have it all, nor should we dwell on what's lost. That's just life—beautiful in its imperfections. And maybe that's the very thing we should be grateful for, because within those imperfections lie endless surprises and new chances to choose again.

We often get caught up in the little things—arguing over who's right or wrong, brooding over mistakes, or letting our pride simmer quietly when someone hurts our feelings. It's all part of being human. I often tell my friends that *I'm just one man in a vast city.* We're all small and solitary in our own way, yet somehow still full of pride. And sometimes, it feels like no one truly understands us—not even ourselves.

But whenever we can, we should take av moment to pause and step back—to observe ourselves from a distance, to be honest about our flaws, and to learn to forgive ourselves. We need sincerity, a bit of compassion, and perhaps a promise or two to do better.

Let every new day begin with fresh energy, a passion for life, and an eagerness to smile. *Let's smile more—me, myself, and all of us.*

## 2. THE STRANGEST THING ABOUT LIFE

A few books have been my lifelong companions. One of them is the Indian epic, *The Mahabharata*. Whenever life gives me a breather, I find myself returning to its pages.

In an old, worn notebook that traveled with me all the way to Europe during my student days, I scribbled down these lines:

*What saves us from danger?* Boldness does. (And maybe a bit of luck, but mostly boldness.)

*What do we need to become wiser?* Not memorizing every page of the Scriptures—but by making friends with the best minds. (You know, the kind who challenge you, yet still manage to buy you a beer after.)

*What supports us and is more noble than the Earth?* Our parents. They brought us into this world, raised us, and somehow resisted the urge to return us for a refund. That makes them more noble than the Earth itself.

*What is higher than the skies?* A father. (Or at least, he certainly thinks so.)

*What is faster than the wind?* Thought. (Particularly when it's a flash of panic about something embarrassing you did ten years ago.)

*What is drier than dry straw?* A heart full of pain. (And yet, it still manages to make the strongest people grow.)

*What keeps people company?* Wisdom. (Though sometimes it's just Netflix.)

*Who is your best friend at home?* Your wife. (Because honestly, she knows where everything is—including your sanity.)

*What is happiness?* Happiness is the result of moral behavior. (And occasionally, a well-timed nap.)

*What is it that, if you give it up, people will love you more?* Arrogance. (Turns out, being humble is a lot more charming.)

*What is it that losing brings you happiness instead of sadness?* Anger. (Once you let go of it, life is surprisingly lighter.)

*What is the strangest thing about life?* We all know we're inching, ever so slowly, towards the end. Yet, everyone alive would trade just about anything for the chance to live forever. Now, isn't that the strangest thing?

# 3. WHAT IS MEDITATION?

Although I was over 40, I often caught myself doing wrong. Age doesn't automatically come with wisdom—it's just a little slower getting caught. I still had character defects: a lack of self-control, a tendency to get frustrated too easily, and I was an expert at finding excuses to dodge personal commitments. You name it—I probably delayed it, even when it was something for my own good.

In late 2005, while traveling through the countryside and the mountains, I paused. Not just to rest, but to think. I realized it was time for a reboot. My brainchild, *Self-Improvement: The Way to the Good, the True, and the Beautiful*, was born in those moments between trips. It was my way of reshaping myself and sharing these ideas with others.

During my life, I've come to understand that meditation is more than just sitting quietly. It's one of the most powerful ways to boost your creativity. And by creativity, I don't just mean coming up with the next great invention—I'm talking about personal enlightenment, a way of shining a new light on life itself. It's about waking up to a higher awareness.

That said, I still haven't mastered everything. Anger? Still working on it. Unfinished tasks? Got a list a mile long. And the Good, the True, and the Beautiful? They're still off in the distance. But here's the thing—it's all part of the process. I'm like a curious student, eager to learn something new every day. Where I was once 70% madness and 30% contemplation, those numbers have flipped. Now, I live more in the quiet space of reflection.

There are countless definitions of meditation, but for me, it's simple. Meditation is living every moment to the fullest. Sure, the Buddha taught us about reincarnation and the Noble Eightfold Path out of suffering, but honestly, I have no clue who I was in my past life—or who I'll be in the next. Confucius once said, "What you don't know isn't your fault." He also mentioned that if we can't fully understand this world, we probably shouldn't worry too much about the next one.

The Buddha gave us some solid advice about living in the now:

*Do not dwell on the past. Do not dream of the future. Concentrate the mind on the present moment. Your countenance is beautiful.*

*(Samyutta Nikaya, Sheaves of Reeds)*

Here's the thing about living in the present: When we're stuck dreaming of the future or lamenting the past, we wither away—just like a reed that parts from its roots. Every moment we let slip through our fingers brings us closer to the grave, but living fully in the present gives each moment a shot at eternity.

If we don't live positively, we lose everything that's precious. We lose our time, our competence, and our wisdom—all the things we need to create inner peace and happiness. That's when life starts to feel dull, and our countenance, well, it withers like a reed.

The Buddha also reminded us not to get too hung up on what's past or what's ahead:

*Do not recollect the past. Nor desire the future. The past is over. The future has not come. These things of the present, see them with insight as they arise.*

*(Majjhima Nikāya III, Anandabhaddekaratta Sutta)*

Worrying about what's behind us or what might be ahead is a waste of time. It drains our energy, leaving us with nothing to give to the present moment—the only moment we truly have.

And then there's the timeless truth the Buddha shared: If you want to stand firm like an island in the middle of a great river or be an island in the ocean, rely on yourself—not on others. The Buddha taught us that the "*Now*" and the "*Here*" are the only safe islands we have. It's the place we can live without drowning in the oceans of depression and delusion.

Ultimately, the way to happiness and peace starts with self-cultivation. It's about training ourselves, upholding pure precepts, and making small efforts every day. Doing the things that keep our minds fresh, like meditating and keeping our focus on the here and now.

In the end, the world we live in matters most. I want to live fully in it, embracing all that it has to offer. By following the Buddha's teachings, I strive to walk the noble path—doing good things every day, even if they're small. Because those small things add up, and they're what lead us to *the Good, the True, and the Beautiful.*

# 4. THE WAY TO THE BUDDHA

As a child, I was scared of the Buddha. Every Sunday, my family would visit my grandma in a quiet neighborhood. To get there, we had to navigate narrow, twisting lanes that seemed to be consumed by wildflowers and tall grass—like something straight out of a haunted tale. When we reached her crumbling doorstep, made of cracked bricks that had probably seen better centuries, my dad would call out softly, "Mom? You home? We've come with the kids." Silence. Then, after a pause, he'd try again. Finally, a raspy voice would echo back from within the house: "Here I am. Come on in." I'd cling to my mom's shirttail, utterly terrified, as my dad nudged open the creaky wooden door that probably hadn't been oiled since the Buddha's own childhood.

Inside, the house was dim even on the brightest of days, as if the walls were afraid of light. My eyes would always need a moment to adjust before I could make out my grandma, sitting on her bed near the window, sewing in the faint light that trickled through. But it was the middle room that unnerved me the most. There, in the deepest part of the house, a few rays of sunlight would sneak through the roof, casting eerie shadows on an altar filled with statues. These statues always looked odd to me, like they were frozen in a contest to see who could look the weirdest. The incense bowls and dusty offerings didn't help either. I was too scared to look too closely—I was convinced one of those statues would blink back at me.

On special days—New Year's, or the first and fifteenth of the lunar month—my family would gather around that altar, hands clasped in prayer. But I was more focused on hiding behind my mom's back than paying attention to any spiritual matters. During meals, grandma would spin tales of Buddha, the Dharma, and the terrifying punishments awaiting those who strayed from the path—limbs chopped off by demons, bodies plunged into boiling cauldrons of oil. As a kid, that was all I needed to never touch a cookie before dinner. I even cracked a tooth once, biting down too hard on my bowl in fear of her stories.

Still, grandma had a certain magic about her. She spoke in this lilting, almost musical way, whether she was talking to neighbors, the chickens, or even the stray dogs that wandered by. She seemed to live in her own world, a place few could enter—except for the butterflies and dragonflies that hovered around her, seemingly unbothered by her spooky tales.

The day before I left to study abroad, I stood outside her house, unsure if I should go in. Eventually, I did. She handed me some dried food and gave me one last warning: "Be good, or else you might meet the devils." Her words stuck with me—not exactly the kind of goodbye Hallmark cards are made of.

By the time I returned home after studying in an Eastern European country, she had passed away. Life wasn't easy then. Sometimes I'd take my mom to the local temple. Sometimes I'd wait outside, guarding the bike like some kind of noble temple sentinel. Other times, I'd venture inside, walking past the red and black statues that still gave me the creeps. Even with a doctorate, I wasn't much closer to understanding Buddha's teachings—or getting over my childhood fear of those statues.

At first, my degree didn't help me much in life. I ended up dabbling in fortune-telling and astrology—not exactly a stable career choice. One day, after yet another financial setback, I went to borrow my brother's motorbike. His response? "How can someone so educated still come here to bother us, borrowing this and that?" Ouch. That was my wake-up call. I decided to switch gears and dive into the world of trading.

I threw myself into the hustle, selling typewriters, photocopiers, and computers, shipping goods across borders—anything to make ends meet. I worked just as hard as I had back in school, but after two years, I was still flat broke. I returned to my dusty, cobweb-filled house—bought with help from my family, who clearly feared I'd end up living in their basement forever. On the table was a moldy letter from my wife, who had moved back in with her parents and left behind a divorce petition. Lovely.

Divorce wasn't exactly new to us; we'd written so many petitions over the years that we probably could've started a paper company. This time, though, I was weirdly okay with it. I had bigger plans on my mind—like heading back to Eastern Europe to try my luck again.

When I arrived, the market economy was in full chaos mode. Inflation was through the roof, goods were scarce, and people were scrambling to survive. I moved to a smaller town, hoping it would be easier to navigate. One night, before yet another business trip, I overheard my friend's wife whispering a prayer: "I'm praying to God and the Buddha… may he have a safe and successful trip." Her words struck a chord with me. From that day on, I began setting up incense bowls wherever I lived, praying before every big decision. It gave me a sense of peace and purpose that I didn't even know I needed.

When I eventually returned home, I brought the practice back with me. I set up altars in every company I worked for. On the first and fifteenth of every month, my colleagues and I would burn incense and make offerings. It became a shared ritual. We even visited temples together, where monks often invited me in for tea and discussions about Buddhism.

Slowly but surely, I started to understand something: the Buddha wasn't someone to fear. He was compassionate and wise, and his teachings were there to guide us to a better life. One day, a monk handed me the Ten Commandments of Buddhism. The first line hit me like a ton of bricks: "Don't wish for a life without difficulties, for without challenges, desires won't be curbed. Don't wish for an easy life, or arrogance will rise." It was like a light bulb went off in my head. I realized I hadn't been living according to Buddha's teachings nearly as well as I thought.

Little by little, I grew closer to the Buddha. I finally dared to look at his face—calm, kind, and understanding. I could almost feel him smile when I did something right, and frown when I veered off course. Gradually, I came to understand that the Buddha wasn't just a distant figure on an altar. He was within me, quietly guiding me along the way.

I shared these revelations with my friends and colleagues. To my surprise, they were eager to learn more. Eventually, I began writing about Buddhism and compiled a series of teachings. It opened up a whole new chapter in my life. My company, my friends, and I grew closer as we followed the Buddha's teachings together.

Even now, whenever I light incense, I feel that same sense of peace that I've come to cherish. The Buddha is there, reminding me that the journey is just as important as the destination, and that every challenge is simply another opportunity to grow.

## 5. PRAYERS TO THE BUDDHA

*I pray to you, Buddha, the Enlightened One. Grant me the strength to endure hardship, and the wisdom to face danger with clarity and courage.*

*I pray to you, Buddha, the Enlightened One. Help me resist the pull of material pleasures and teach me the art of self-discipline.*

*I pray to you, Buddha, the Enlightened One. Show me the way to overcome obstacles, to persevere, and to never give up—because every challenge is an opportunity for growth.*

*I pray to you, Buddha, the Enlightened One. Give me the strength to be humble, to forgive, and to remain true to myself, while extending kindness and goodwill to others.*

*I pray to you, Buddha, the Enlightened One. Teach me to appreciate life as it is, to remember that simplicity is a gift, and that true power lies in benevolence.*

# 6. FIRST DAYS IN A FOREIGN LAND

I arrived in Los Angeles one Saturday afternoon after a nearly 24-hour flight that left me exhausted and a little dazed. After a few more hours of travel, I finally reached the small town where I'd be staying. Settled into my room, I decided to do a trial run from my hotel to the university. I was about to start my studies at the H-School at UC Berkeley. Funny how life works—I had once studied physics in the USSR, where we referenced work from Berkeley's famous high-energy physics lab and its Compact Particle Accelerator. But here I was, not heading to the Physics Department, but to H-School. I had never studied business formally before.

Before leaving the hotel, I asked the receptionist how long it would take to get to campus. She casually replied, "About 10 minutes." Seemed easy enough. However, after walking for what felt like miles without a university in sight, I began to think that "10 minutes" meant something entirely different to her. I asked for directions multiple times, scaled some steep hills, but still, no H-School. Starving and frustrated, I was about to turn back when I stumbled upon some food shops—a lifesaver for a single, older student like me. By the time I returned to my hotel, the sun was setting. I bought a tray of Thai food for $6, microwaved it, and soon my room was filled with the comforting aroma of slightly burnt black bread. Delicious.

The next day, a Sunday, I had a meet-and-greet scheduled at H-School at 6 p.m. Determined not to repeat my earlier adventure, I left at 4 p.m. Dashing past bookstores and crowded pubs, I weaved through students laughing and chatting. My feet were sore, but excitement pushed me forward. Luckily, another student took pity on me and guided me to campus. The campus was even more beautiful than I had imagined—a massive complex under green canopies, far more impressive than I expected.

When I arrived at the reception area, it was bustling with familiar faces from NTU in Singapore, where we had studied together the previous year. There were also new faces, mostly from the U.S. and neighboring countries. After a few rounds of introductions—complete with wine—we parted ways. Two new friends, one from India and one from Hong Kong, were staying at the same hotel, so we decided to walk back together.

Our first mission was to find SIM cards. The guy from Hong Kong assured us he knew the cheapest option, and though my feet were killing me, I followed along. After securing our phone lines, we found a cozy Mexican restaurant for dinner. The warm, busy atmosphere inside was a welcome contrast to the chilly spring air outside. Coal fireplaces flickered in the corners, and the waiters darted around like ninjas. I found a perfect spot to observe all the action.

As we waited for our food, we got to know each other better. The guy from Hong Kong worked in express delivery and managed my country's market, though, ironically, he had never actually been there. The Indian guy, a bulky yet friendly fellow, worked in oil and gas and had visited my country a few times. When the food arrived, I realized I'd made a mistake. Thanks to my poor English, I had accidentally ordered vegetarian. Meanwhile, my friends were enjoying heaps of grilled meat that made my mouth water.

"Are you a vegetarian?" the guy from Hong Kong asked, eyeing my plate.

"Yes... a few days a week, especially Sundays," I replied sheepishly.

"Good timing then!" he laughed, before diving back into his mountain of meat.

After a glass of beer, my resolve weakened, and I found myself eyeing the meat hungrily. I said, "Isn't it strange? India was the cradle of Buddhism, yet it's hardly there anymore."

The Indian guy, his mouth full of chicken, nodded. "That's true. Just like Israel was the cradle of Christianity, but now... not so much."

The conversation shifted to monks and Tibetan Buddhism. I mentioned that some monks in Tibet are allowed to marry and even eat meat freely.

"Is that true?" asked the guy from Hong Kong, pausing his meal.

"Yep. I've read and seen pictures about it," I replied confidently.

"Well, that's cool!" they both exclaimed, digging back into their meals.

We finished our food and, with full bellies and satisfied smiles, decided to continue our conversation over drinks. The evening turned into a sort of brotherhood— eating vegetarian and drinking wine felt like a gathering straight out of *Water Margin.*

Over the next two weeks, we three ate dinner together almost every night, working our way through the restaurants along the street where we stayed. I had originally planned to save money by microwaving meals in my room, but thanks to my friends, eating out became the norm. It was a relief that the economic downturn seemed to be hitting the U.S. more slowly than my country—dinners cost around ten dollars, which was much cheaper than hosting guests at home.

We shared taxis to school every morning and afternoon, and I later found out that my Hong Kong friend had called his wife after our first night together. He told her about his "poor friend from my country" who walked thirty minutes to school and ate vegetarian to save money. His wife suggested he invite me to share cab rides and meals. Poor me! To hell with my bad English! In trying to save face, I ended up spending more money eating out and taking taxis than I'd planned, all while insisting on splitting the bills evenly.

One night, after a few glasses of wine, I decided to share my philosophy on self-cultivation—my *True, Good, and Beautiful* model, and the concept of BHMS (Body, Heart, Mind, Spirit). I used more hand gestures than necessary, but my Hong Kong friend seemed genuinely interested. The next day, he told me he had spent nearly two hours explaining my philosophy to his wife, though she found it hard to understand. "Why do you tell your wife everything?" I laughed, shaking my head.

By the second week, I discovered my knack for leadership. During a particularly challenging group project, I managed to assign tasks based on each person's strengths. Rana, a brilliant Singaporean student, handled the slides, while the others focused on calculations and market analysis. By the end of the day, we had a polished presentation, while other groups were still stuck in arguments.

On our last day, my Hong Kong friend insisted on changing his flight to sit next to me. We talked non-stop during the flight, like old friends reluctant to say goodbye. At the Hong Kong airport, he told me, "The best lesson I've learned here is your BHMS model. The rest at H-School? Not so interesting." We laughed, but his words stayed with me.

After returning to my country, I was quickly caught up in work. A few days later, I visited a doctor because my arm had been hurting ever since my time at H-School. The doctor pressed on my arm and asked, "Have you been eating lots of seafood and drinking wine?"

"Well... yeah. It was cheap," I admitted.

"First time it's hurt like this?"

"Yeah."

"Early gout, buddy. Watch out for the wine and crustaceans."

No more wine and shrimp? Impossible! I could give up shrimp, maybe even crabs—but wine? As I massaged my aching arm, I couldn't help but think of my friend from Hong Kong. I guess I've lost letter B, thanks to him!

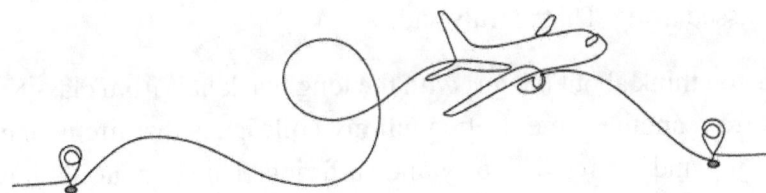

## 7. GOODBYE, SORROW!

Yesterday was one of those sad days. It started early in the morning when I tried, in vain, to light some incense—the lighter had run out of gas. Then, while dashing out the door, I realized I had forgotten an important document at home. Great. On the road, traffic was moving at a snail's pace because the bridge was clogged with cars. And just when I thought it couldn't get worse, my phone rang. Glancing at the number, I figured it was my partner reminding me—yet again—that I needed to make a payment for our contract. As soon as I reached the office, I anxiously opened my email. Bad news: someone wanted to delay paying off a debt they owed us. And naturally, we needed that money—badly.

Life, as we all know, is full of sad stories. It's sad when things don't go our way. It's sad when our family misunderstands or criticizes us. It's sad when a jealous colleague envies us or when we feel like we're losing out. It's sad when a relationship ends. And it's especially sad when you're sick, unable to move, coughing nonstop, while the garden outside is bursting with life. It's sad when you have to live far from home for months, watching your classmates go out to enjoy themselves while you sit alone at the dining table with nothing but your shadow stretching across the lawn in the cold northern light. And school reunions? They're a mixed bag. The yard is full of laughter and familiar faces, but then you notice the few who are missing. Later, you find out some are still wandering the world, while others have passed away. That is truly sad.

It's sad when you think about the girl with the long black hair from class K and her smiling eyes from another time. I often tell my colleagues that life is maybe two or three parts joy and the rest is worry and suffering. Think about it—how many moments of real joy have you had in your life? How many nights have you gone to bed with a smile? And how many years have you spent simply thinking, worrying, and struggling to get by?

Sure, they say the destination is where the joy is. But the truth is, the joy is often short-lived compared to the long, hard struggle it takes to get there. Maybe life is more about pain than pleasure. Sometimes I feel like a mountain goat—excited to climb one peak and enjoy the view, only to spot an even higher mountain and rush down, eager to conquer it too. So sad!

Yesterday was one of those days at work. Slow. Everyone was trying—at least they said they were. Yet, week after week, month after month, nothing seemed to change. There were always excuses: sick kids, house repairs, stomachaches, evening classes, weddings, vacations, heartbreaks, or needing to leave early because their significant other was threatening to break up. During a meeting, I admitted I was feeling sad, but I couldn't pinpoint why. Six months had passed— what had we accomplished? What needed to change?

Someone suggested a 360-degree assessment of me as part of our six-month review. Another colleague, who had gone with me to the Department of Business where I give lectures sometimes, remarked that I seemed to have a better face there—less frustrated, easier to get along with. So sad... I made a note of that. If a 360-degree assessment would help, we'd do it immediately. And if replacing my "unacceptable face" with a constant smile would somehow make people finish their work, then sure, I'd make the change. But as I thought about it, I realized: I had been away for three months, and nothing had changed. People still had stomachaches, still repaired their houses, still argued about love, and still left work early because someone was waiting for them. Life goes on.

Another evening, still feeling down, I went to watch a Korean drum performance. I'd made some Korean friends through work, and we had visited each other a few times. I always believed my country's culture was more diverse and nuanced. We seemed more sophisticated—at least, that's what I thought.

But that night, a delegation from my country joined the event. Our girls were beautiful, with inviting eyes and smiles like blossoming flowers. They danced gracefully, their arms and legs moving deliberately. But when I compared them to the Korean dancers, it was like night and day. Our girls trotted across the stage, while the Koreans seemed to glide effortlessly, like the wind. Their movements were fluid and elegant, full of energy and color. Our dancers, though smiling beautifully, sometimes forgot their steps.

It made me reflect. Why are we, with our rich history and heroic culture, not on par with other nations in times of peace? Why were we unstoppable in war but struggle to find our footing during peace? It's a tough question.

I brought back over a hundred kilos of books and documents from the U.S., and while knowledge fills my mind, the most important lesson is our commitment to work and life. I don't know who you are or where you're from, but whatever path you've chosen, don't complain or make excuses. Fulfill your responsibilities in the simplest, most creative way possible. Innovate constantly to make life exciting and inspiring. And do it today, right now, in this moment. Every moment counts because once it's gone, it's gone for good. So treasure every one of them. If you do, your commitment will embody the spirit of Bushido.

Where are you, sorrow? The Buddha taught that life is impermanent. Birth, old age, sickness, and death are as natural as the seasons. After joy comes sorrow—and there is far more sorrow than joy. How can you escape pain and illness when life changes with every second? How can you detach from joy, sorrow, anger, and jealousy when those around you are consumed by them? The truth is, you can't. But the choices you make leave a mark on your life.

Your journey will be full of unexpected twists, lucky breaks, separations, spans of happiness, rivers of doubt, waterfalls of jealousy, reefs of intrigue, and the loneliness of strange seas. These are just some of the endless forms of human sorrow that we all must face.

Don't run from any of it. Meet it with patience, restraint, and even a bit of foolishness. No matter how strong or weak, wise or naive you are, accept sorrow along with everything else. See each step as a new challenge, brimming with life, creativity, and opportunity. Make it fun—if you can.

And remember, the destination is just a place to rest when you're a bit tired from the long road. It's a momentary pause, a brief farewell to the weariness of the journey. But once you've rested, get back on track because the road ahead never ends. If you can do that, you'll find more joy than sorrow, and sorrow itself will become fleeting.

So don't hesitate. Say to yourself, "Goodbye, sorrow! I'll keep on going now."

## 8. ROSES AND THORNS

*This world is neither all roses nor all thorns. The rose is soft, beautiful, and fragrant. But the stem it grows on is lined with thorns. What's rosy remains rosy, and what's thorny remains thorny. You don't avoid the rose just because of the thorns, and you don't dismiss the rose because the thorns exist.*

*Like the ever-swinging pendulum, life constantly shifts between opposites. There are four conditions in life that everyone, without exception, will face at some point: gain and loss, fame and infamy, praise and blame, happiness and pain.*

*When things go wrong or when life is full of joy and ups and downs, there's one thing you can always do: maintain a balanced mind.*

*(Eight Worldly Conditions, Th e Buddha and His Teachings-Venerable Narada Maha Thera)*

## 9. LET ME GO HOME!

This is it. In just a few minutes, I'll be leaving this room on the HBS campus (Harvard Business School), a place that has been my home for almost three months. And what a wild three months it's been! The ups and downs of this time have been more intense, more profound than my entire student life. This experience has changed me at a deeper level.

Now, the room is clean and empty. But just a few days ago, it was a disaster zone— books, notebooks, clothes, documents, and random personal belongings scattered everywhere. I even sent home over 10 packages of books and papers (I lost count somewhere around package number five). Every day, I'd hear the doors creaking open around me and knew that the students next door were off for their morning exercise. Not wanting to be left behind, I'd throw on my shoes and join them. That was the start of each day—a new day with hundreds of challenges waiting.

Ten weeks flew by in the blink of an eye, filled with a rollercoaster of emotions. Stress? Check. Language barriers? Check. Drowning in documents? Oh, definitely check. Sometimes, it felt like I couldn't breathe, like I was sinking and would be forced to drop out of the race. But somehow, I always found a way to calm myself. I would take a deep breath, learn something new, and pick up speed again. There were arguments, discoveries, breakthroughs—it felt just like my student days all over again, only this time with much higher stakes.

Yesterday was graduation, and the ceremony was unforgettable. The farewell dinner was moving, with everyone feeling a mix of joy and nostalgia. As I looked around, I realized that my classmates had gone through the same struggles I had. No one talked about it, but you could see it in their eyes. We had all endured the early days of stress and uncertainty, but we came out the other side—together. Every day, we walked the same path, not leaving anyone behind.

One of our classmates even broke his leg playing football. He was in the hospital for three days, but when he came back, he rolled into class in a wheelchair like nothing had happened. He didn't miss a single lecture. You could see the determination in his eyes as he navigated the halls and stairs, and we all gave him our encouragement. That resilience, that unwavering commitment, was something I admired deeply. I learned a lot from my professors, but I learned just as much from my classmates.

And now, here I am, about to leave this room. I turned on my small radio, a comforting companion during these months, and a song came on that stopped me in my tracks:

*"Another sunny day,*

*Has come and gone away...*

*Maybe surrounded by,*

*A million people I,*

*Still feel all alone,*

*I just want to go home...".*   *(Home! - Westlife)*

The song hit me right in the chest. Sure, the last three months have been amazing, full of challenges and surprises, but the truth is, I want to go home. We said our goodbyes yesterday, but there was a silent plea in their eyes that said, "Don't leave." It's been incredible here, but I miss my friends, my colleagues, my family. Home is calling. I've got to go home.

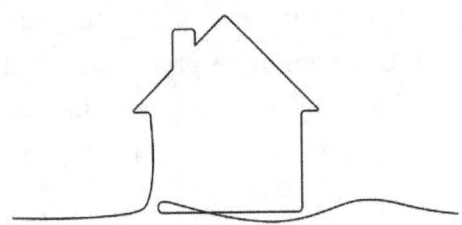

## 10. HUMAN BEINGS AND PERFECTION

For nearly 3,000 years, humans have been contemplating the meaning of life. We've been trying to understand ourselves, the universe, and how to align with Nature. From ancient Greece to modern-day China, from Israel to India, sages like Plato, Confucius, Buddha, and Einstein—despite expressing their thoughts in different ways—have essentially agreed on one thing: the four fundamental elements of a human being. These elements are the **Body**, **Mind**, **Heart**, and **Spirit**. In simpler terms: our physical self, intellect, emotions, and beliefs. Let's call it the BIEM model.

Similarly, society reflects these four dimensions: **material**, **knowledge**, **emotion**, and **belief**. The connections between us and society are strong—together, they shape our destiny.

Let's break this down a little further.

Consider your own body. You're a walking universe. Did you know you've got over 40 trillion cells in you? That's more than thousands of times the world's population. Each cell is made up of billions of molecules, and each molecule contains atoms equal to the total number of stars in ten thousand universes. Think about that! In terms of composition, you're bigger than the universe. That's some serious stuff, right?

But just being aware of this is not enough. The trick is to align these elements within yourself. As humans, our history isn't just about wars, peace, successes, and failures. It's also about our evolution in awareness, constantly growing, shifting. You—me—each of us is a little universe. And the better we understand ourselves, the better we understand the larger universe we're all part of. So let's take a look at each element:

*1. Body*

Your body is your temple, your vehicle. It thrives or suffers based on how you treat it. When it comes to physical health, we're talking about opposites: "healthy, lively, elegant" vs. "weak, lazy, sluggish."

Across cultures, one thing is clear: a healthy body is good; an unhealthy body is not. It doesn't matter whether you're rich or poor—disease comes from a lack of understanding. It's sad but true. People rarely care about others when they're healthy, but the moment you fall ill, they send you gifts you can't even use. If you truly love someone, don't just shower them with flowers when they're sick—teach them how to avoid sickness altogether.

**So how do you keep your body in harmony with Nature?**

**Eat wisely** and adjust your habits over time.

**Exercise regularly**—and that doesn't mean running a marathon every day. Just move, keep active in ways that suit your body and age.

**Balance your life**—live, work, and rest in harmony.

**Be happy with what you have.** Contentment is key.

When your body is healthy, it fuels the other three elements. But when you're ill, your mind gets clouded, your emotions dim, and your spirit darkens.

*2. Mind*

The mind is your tool for analysis, creativity, and imagination. It's what helps you make sense of the world. Most of us did the heavy lifting for our minds when we were in school, but here's the kicker: much of what you learn in school doesn't actually help you at work. The world changes fast, and lifelong learning is essential.

**How do you nurture your mind?**

**Learn continuously.** Make learning a habit—schedule time every day to read, think, and explore new ideas.

**Practice creativity.** Keep a journal of ideas, brainstorm freely, and engage in creative thinking.

**Teach and share knowledge.** Teaching is one of the best ways to deepen your understanding.

When the mind is underdeveloped, life gets harder. Ignorance can lead to poor health, social awkwardness, and a lack of passion or purpose. A perfect mind is a curious mind—always studying, always creating.

*3. Heart*

The heart is where your emotions live, and how you interact with the world emotionally shapes your success. Sometimes, the most intelligent people struggle emotionally. Social awareness, empathy, and self-awareness are just as important as intellect.

**How do you develop emotional intelligence?**

**Know yourself.** Reflect on your desires, your passions, and your ideals.

**Adapt and grow.** Work on your emotional flaws day by day, making small improvements.

**Empathize.** Listen to others, understand them, and find common ground.

An emotionally balanced person is resilient, passionate, and connected. Someone emotionally out of balance risks losing not just their mental clarity but their health and spirit too.

*4. Spirit*

Your spirit is what drives everything else. It's the part of you that believes in something greater, that connects you to eternity. When the body fades and the mind forgets, the spirit remains. It guides your conscience, helps you live with purpose, and connects you to something beyond yourself.

**How do you nurture your spirit?**

- **Live a life of righteousness.** Do the right thing, avoid dishonesty, and act with nobility.

- **Contribute to the world.** Live meaningfully and give back.

- **Build inner strength.** Live humbly, with depth, avoiding superficial vanity.

*The Equation of Life*

Most of us aren't perfect in all four areas. You may know an athlete with a perfect body, a scientist with a sharp mind, an artist with rich emotions, or a monk with strong beliefs. But rarely does someone excel in all four. Yet, when the four elements do converge—magic happens. Think of Einstein, whose thoughts paralleled the Buddha's. Beethoven, who combined artistic brilliance with missionary strength. Miyamoto Musashi, a master swordsman and artist who lived in harmony with nature and spirit.

For leaders, it's crucial to nurture all four elements—your organization's long-term success depends on it. For the rest of us, focusing on these four areas can lead to a fuller, happier life.

# 11. THE EQUATION OF LIFE

Years of reflecting on my own character flaws have brought me to this point of understanding. It's a journey I call "Self-development: The Way to the True, the Good, and the Beautiful." This process has required immense effort and commitment from both my heart and mind. If I had written everything down initially, the first draft could have been a hefty book. But, through teaching and sharing these ideas with others, I've learned more along the way. Perfection, it seems, is always ahead of us, and the road toward it feels limitless. Though I've spent time pondering my shortcomings, I now have a clearer direction.

In the book, *Your Dream Will Come True Without Fail* (which I gave to each of my colleagues, though I have no idea if anyone's actually read it), the author Imamura Kazuo—President of Kyocera Corporation—presents a formula for success in life:

**Success in life = Ability × Passion × Mindset**

*Equation (1)*

The conclusion is simple: you can't lead a great life with moderate ability, lack of passion, and a negative mindset.

It's a solid formula, but I believe it can be refined further. Drawing from the model of human dimensions, I propose this adjustment:

**B** (Body) = Health

**H** (Heart) = Enthusiasm

**M** (Mind) = Intelligence

**S** (Spirit) = Belief

With this in mind, I suggest an updated equation:

**Success in life = F(B, M, H, S) = B × M × H × S**

*Equation (2)*

Each of these elements has a potential score from 0 to 10. In an ideal world, a perfect person would score 10 in all four elements. So, the equation for the ultimate human being would be:

**Success in life** $= 10 \times 10 \times 10 \times 10 = 10,000$.

Both equations work similarly, but my version separates health as a distinct parameter. In Kazuo's equation, intelligence is included under ability. I believe it's worth distinguishing these elements to capture the true complexity of life.

Let's break down the scores:

**Health**: $\{0,10\}$

**Intelligence**: $\{0,10\}$

**Enthusiasm**: $\{0,10\}$

**Belief**: $\{-10,10\}$

Let me elaborate a bit more on this. Your ability might be something you've inherited genetically—thank your parents for that. But enthusiasm and health are cultivated through practice. To reach perfection, things like harmony, faith, and depth are built up over time, often by adults who've learned the value of balance. Meanwhile, belief isn't just a thing you have; it's your perspective on life. Some people pursue noble causes, while others get tangled in envy or ambition at others' expense. This explains why belief can range from -10 to 10. A person's score in life, then, can go negative if they allow destructive beliefs to take root.

In life, success is a multiplication of four elements: health, intelligence, enthusiasm, and belief. Low intelligence can be balanced out by higher levels of passion, faith, or a strong work ethic. Good health and a strong desire to learn can lift someone higher than raw intelligence alone. This is the pathway to achieving the highest level of success.

**The formula for a perfect life might look something like this:**

**B** = Health (Perfect B = Health + Harmony)

**M** = Intelligence (Perfect M = Study + Creativity)

**H** = Emotion (Perfect H = Passion + Faith)

**S** = Spirit (Perfect S = Profoundness + Nobility)

Thus, the equation of life opens a new path:

$$BMHS = F(BMHS) \rightarrow F(perfect\ BMHS) = True - Good - Beautiful$$
*Equation (3)*

This is the journey toward self-development and, ultimately, toward perfection in life: embodying the True, the Good, and the Beautiful in every aspect of our lives.

# 12. ADMONISHING OURSELVES, ADMONISHING OTHERS

I had to mull this over for a while before continuing. Some things, after all, are personal—too private, even—but to get from a dark path to an enlightened one, sometimes you need to shed light on the uncomfortable. I want to find shelter in Buddhism, where righteousness is the foundation of the Dharma.

The Buddha didn't bark orders or punish his disciples for not following a set of rigid rules. Instead, he laid out the law of cause and effect—karma—and showed the way to enlightenment. He offered principles for nurturing virtues and finding the right path, but Buddhists aren't forced into rigid "taboos." We can choose our own way. The Buddha himself said that Arhats and Bodhisattvas are only guides who've found release from suffering. They walk the path of truth and have the kindness to help others who seek it. Listening to the Buddha's teachings, I've found, is a must for inner peace, serenity, and sustainable success in life and work. The foundation? The Five Precepts. Let me share them.

## 1. Abstaining from Killing

This precept is about avoiding harm. No one has the right to take life—whether it's a human, an animal, or even the smallest creature. The Buddha's compassion extends to all living things, which is why monks in the pagoda often stay indoors during the spring to avoid stepping on tiny life bursting forth in bloom. The Buddha said, *"Scary are the clubs and swords, love all living buds, live a hungry life, be in another's shoes, do not kill or incite to kill."*

But does this mean no meat on your plate? Not necessarily. Theravada Buddhism never forbade eating meat. If it was offered, monks could eat it. Some sects, like those in China, Japan, and other parts of Asia, avoid it, but others, like Mikkyo in Tibet, don't impose such restrictions. In fact, a Mikkyo monk once said that slaughtering a sheep to save a village was better than eating a pile of vegetables that led to the deaths of countless tiny insects.

For me, giving up meat is more practical than noble. I'm dealing with gout—one more perk of getting older—so I've quit eating shrimp and crab. I figure this saves a few animals, but honestly, it's just better for my health. Instead of fish sauce, I've got rice, tofu, veggies, and peanuts on my plate. Now, when I walk, I'm careful not to step on worms or ants, and I teach my kids to love the trees and not catch

43

butterflies in the garden. But, if I'm being honest, mosquitoes and flies...well, they're my downfall. So, I'm pledging to stop swatting. I'll just let them bite me and call it karma.

## 2. Abstaining from Theft

This one's about taking what isn't yours, no matter how big or small. Theft can take many forms—stealing money, time, even ideas. The Buddha said, *"Avoid taking what isn't yours, no matter where you are, in the jungle or a deserted village. If something belongs to another, don't even think of making it yours."*

I've tried to live by this principle for over 40 years. I haven't cheated anyone out of money or goods, and although I've faced false accusations a few times, I walk with my head held high. I've never looked down on anyone else's possessions. That said, I might have stolen a few books from secondhand shops as a kid, and I may have forgotten to return library books on occasion. But as Sir Isaac Newton once said, we stand on the shoulders of giants, and I often tell my students that the only theft allowed is the theft of knowledge.

## 3. Avoiding Sensual Misconduct

The Buddha's take on relationships was simple: Keep things virtuous and avoid getting tangled in lust. He taught, *"One should abstain from sensual misconduct and avoid relationships with those protected by parents, siblings, relatives, or those already spoken for."*

The precept helps preserve family peace and builds trust between partners. Let's just say that if I messed up here in my younger years, I now ask for forgiveness. The philosopher Osho once said, *"Live your youth to the fullest. If you fully live in the moment, you won't have to worry about the future."*

I think he's right. I've lived my youth, and now in my 40s, I've entered a more reflective phase. I reread the Buddha's words on sensuality and take a deep breath. I've got a family of four beloved kids, and that's more than enough for me. I don't need to cross any more lines.

## 4. Abstaining from False Speech

Words have power—far more than we often realize. The Buddha urged us to avoid lies, slander, rude language, and frivolous talk. He said, *"A bhikkhu does*

44

*not lie. He speaks sincerely, without misleading others, and his heart is full of trustworthiness. He never uses words to divide or deceive, but only to unite and build peace."*

When I was younger, I had a sharp tongue. I grew up on a business street, and let's just say I wasn't always well-behaved. But life—and some gifted friends—set me straight. Still, I've had my moments. Have you ever said something in anger that you regretted for years afterward? I have.

That's why I've learned to control my words. Less boasting, more humility. I keep the Buddha's teachings nearby to remind myself to watch my tongue. But it's tough. Just yesterday, I called an employee an idiot. I regretted it instantly. Sorry, dude! (I'll make sure to place the Five Precepts by my bed, so they're the first thing I see when I wake up.)

## 5. Abstaining from Fermented Drinks That Cause Heedlessness

And here we are—wine, beer, and spirits. How could we live without them? How could we express our sincerity without a drink? Wine washes away homesickness and brings friends closer. But the Buddha warned that drinking too much leads to heedlessness—bad decisions, broken rules, and the loss of everything we've worked to build.

I'm guilty of this. When I drink, I drink to the last drop. This often leads to a violation of several precepts at once—especially the first three. The animal inside me takes over, and who knows what might happen next? But that was yesterday. I'm older now and stick to light wine, the kind that's good for your health. I tell my wife to pick me up when I've had too much, just to keep things in check.

Still, I can't quit entirely. So, I've compromised. I display bottles of wine all over my house—my office, kitchen, and cellar—not to drink, but just to admire. That way, I don't miss the taste but avoid the hangover.

## 13. WHERE ARE YOU, MY COUNTRY'S SPIRIT?

There are some big questions people have been asking for generations: "Who am I?" "Where am I from?" "What am I supposed to do?" and "Where should I go?" Life seems like a series of endless roads that are all connected in some way, each leading us toward answers that might be just around the corner—or a million miles away.

Outside my window is a beautiful garden with vibrant flowers and butterflies flitting around like tiny colorful dancers. And then, suddenly, a yellow leaf falls. Somewhere in the distance, I hear the solemn notes of a funeral. It's a painful reminder that life, no matter how full it seems, is fleeting.

As I was working on my lecture, *"Self-Development: A Path to the True, the Good, and the Beautiful,"* I stumbled upon these words of wisdom:

*"Sow a thought, reap an action.*

*Sow an action, reap a habit.*

*Sow a habit, reap a character.*

*Sow a character, reap a destiny."*

It's all about destiny, and it got me thinking about where we're all headed. Just like the students who recite traditional verses with the rhythm of a marching band, each generation follows the steps of the one before them, creating an eternal flow.

In the past 15 years, my country has seen enormous change. People, young and old, are working tirelessly, pouring their energy into building something better. There's wisdom, passion, and an unwavering faith that, no matter how tough things get, we'll figure it out. But still, I ask myself:

*"Where are you, my country's spirit?*

*Where have we been? Where are we going?"*

Sure, we've accomplished a lot over these past 15 years, but what comes next? The economy is important, but it isn't everything. Material wealth can never replace the deeper essence of culture. Without a strong cultural spirit and a commitment to fostering our unique civilization, we'll never see sustainable growth.

Look at Japan—a country we all admire for its remarkable rise to power. A small island chain with virtually no natural resources, prone to disasters, and yet, it's thrived. Japan went from being a closed-off feudal state to defeating the Tsar's army in World War I. And then, after being reduced to ashes during World War II, it bounced back in less than 30 years to become a global economic powerhouse.

So, what's their secret? How do they hold on to their traditions while racing ahead into modernity, full steam ahead with robots, automated systems, and digital hyper-speed?

In the late 19th century, Japan sent its brightest students to Europe and America to study Western industrial techniques and management methods. When they returned, they brought modernity back with them, but it wasn't a smooth transition. Japan was a nation of contradictions, torn between old and new, tradition and progress.

During this time of upheaval, *Bushido: The Soul of Japan* was published in 1905. This book redefined and reaffirmed the cultural values of Japan. It laid out the philosophy of the samurai, the moral backbone that shaped Japan's national character for centuries. Bushido emphasized self-discipline, loyalty, and personal honor, helping to create the Japan we know today.

It's a reminder that to understand ourselves, we need to understand others. The Japanese have Bushido. My country has a deep respect for filial piety, courtesy, and the Five Constant Virtues, much like the Japanese. But understanding our spirit and identity is a journey that doesn't end, even after 100 years of prosperity.

In 2006, Japanese mathematician Masahiko Fujiwara wrote *The Dignity of a Nation.* The book was a wake-up call, urging Japan to return to the core values of Bushido and reject the Western mindset that prioritizes personal gain above all else. Fujiwara argued that Japan needed to restore compassion, righteousness, faithfulness, bravery, self-improvement, and a sense of duty to the needy. It struck a chord—within a year, two million copies of the book had been sold.

And yet, even the Japanese worry about losing their way. What about us? My country's spirit—where is it? What cultural values can drive us toward sustainable development in this new era?

A nation's destiny is shaped by its character and the paths it chooses. Every country has its own dignity, just like every person has their own character. But what's the right path for my country? This question has haunted me for years.

I'm not a great man—just someone with a deep love for my country. I remind myself that I'm just a tiny grain of sand in this vast world, but I hope that through my learning and exploration, I can contribute something meaningful to my country's future.

Today, as our organization celebrates its 15th anniversary, and as our economy faces turbulent times, I think about the road ahead. I believe the way forward should look like this:

- *Preserve the national spirit, and from that, create a national religion.*

- *Preserve the national religion, and from that, create a thriving culture.*

- *Preserve the thriving culture, and from that, create economic growth.*

- *Preserve economic growth, and from that, create sustainable development.*

My country's people have long viewed Tao, or "The Way," as a guide to moral principles and living a righteous life. But at its core, Tao is about finding the right path. A leader must choose the correct path for their nation, leading it to prosperity while upholding its values. And only with a strong national spirit can we achieve true sustainable development.

I remember a time when I was out for drinks with a Jewish friend of mine. After a few rounds, he said, "Hey J, I feel like I'm in Tel Aviv when I'm here in your city. Your country and mine have so much in common. I feel like you're a Jew, just like me."

I laughed and poured us another drink. We clinked glasses and drank like brothers. After wandering the globe for nearly 3,000 years, the Jewish people finally returned to their homeland. They're not going anywhere now. It's a small population, but they've shaken the Middle East.

I've seen Jewish people everywhere—Russia, Europe, the U.S.—and I've read countless books by Jewish authors. Heck, most of my professors at Harvard were Jewish. Sometimes, I think my business is a plaything in the hands of Jewish investment funds. You're not really kind, dude!

But jokes aside, these people have an unbreakable spirit. And as I sit here thinking about the future of my own country, I wonder: where are we heading?

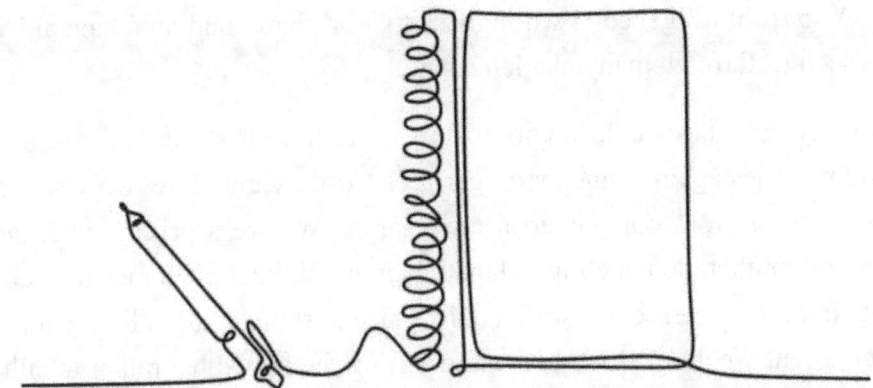

# 14. WHO ARE WE, MY COUNTRY?

When reviewing the development of nations, particularly in East Asia over the past 200 years, it becomes clear that maintaining a country's identity while pursuing economic growth is essential for sustainable development. As citizens of my country, we must understand the core values and qualities we have inherited from our ancestors—values shaped and fortified by centuries of labor, creativity, and fierce defense of our land. It is crucial to preserve the harmony among the different ethnic groups within our country's borders while also embracing the best that the world has to offer. Perhaps our country's finest qualities are as follows:

- National pride and a strong sense of community.

- A deep value for affection, gratitude, and humanity.

- A spirit of diligence, a willingness to work hard, and an adaptability that has seen us through many challenges.

Our country may be small, but its history is rich with stories of wisdom and strategic victories against much stronger foes. At the same time, we've absorbed valuable lessons from our powerful adversaries. We are a people who, despite centuries of conflict, do not cling to fanaticism in religion or embrace unnecessary fighting. In times of peace, we seek a quiet place to settle, make a living, and have many children. We don't strive to stand out from the crowd but rather to cultivate affection and gratitude. We respect harmony and are always ready to work hard. However, once we achieve a level of success, we might get a bit too comfortable and think, *Well, I'm not as high as some, but not as low as others.*

This, perhaps, is where we differ most from our neighbors, such as the Japanese. The Japanese are like the sun: powerful, disciplined, and relentless in their pursuit of perfection. They tackle challenges with a resilience that sometimes pushes them to extremes, whether in times of war or peace. Their samurai traditions may be centuries old, but the spirit of Bushido remains deeply embedded in their culture.

In contrast, we might be more like the moon: soft, content, kind, introspective, and adaptable. Our flexibility is our strength, allowing us to navigate challenges without succumbing to extremes. If anything, we can learn from the Japanese—how to be more determined, detail-oriented, and committed to perfection in building our nation. But just as the Japanese could benefit from a bit of our adaptability, we, too, can grow by adopting some of their drive and meticulousness.

The world is interconnected now, thanks to the Internet. It's a level playing field where our disadvantages can be turned into strengths. Flexibility and adaptability are often highlighted as key traits for success, and it seems we have both in spades. If every citizen, young and old, across our country and in far-off lands, understood that our homeland has been impoverished but is rich in potential, they would be inspired to contribute to its progress and prosperity.

Being poor is not just an economic condition—it's a national disgrace that robs us of our pride. It's the kind of thing that makes us feel ashamed before our ancestors, who fought and bled to protect this land. This isn't just about economic growth; it's about fighting for our nation's honor and dignity. If we embrace this challenge with the creativity and courage of our forebears, we can become one of the world's leading nations in both culture and economy.

Just as Bushido is the soul of Japan, the spirit of our country might be best represented by the worship of the Mother Goddess.

### The Spirit of the Mother Goddess

Religions in our country have deep roots in foreign influences, yet they've been adapted to suit our national spirit. Confucianism and the Tao have long been seen not as religions but as guiding moral principles for self-improvement, righteous living, and service to society. Buddhism, which originated in India, was brought to our country via different paths, and its teachings emphasize benevolence and the avoidance of suffering caused by desires like greed, hate, and ignorance. We don't typically delve into the philosophical depths of Buddhism, but we feel a natural closeness to its teachings and view the Buddha as a benevolent figure.

Christianity arrived in our country in the 16th century and has been embraced by many who trust in the Holy Father and Jesus Christ. Meanwhile, other foreign religions, such as Daoism and Islam, have also found their way here, coexisting with our native spiritual traditions.

But perhaps the most quintessentially local religion is the worship of the Mother Goddess—a practice that emerged as our people sought to highlight our national spirit and preserve what they had earned through centuries of hard work and struggle. Legend tells us that the Mother Goddess descended to Earth three times in different lives, sometimes living by the sea, sometimes in the mountains. She healed the sick, protected the people from oppression and evil spirits, and brought them happiness. In this way, she became like a mother to the people—always present in their lives.

Worship of the Mother Goddess is an epic, beautiful tradition filled with poetry, music, and dramatic performances. At times, it is heroic and powerful, while at others, it is soft and tender. The Mother Goddess is like the force that flows through our rivers and mountains, nurturing our spirit and spreading love throughout our country. Her festivals are grand celebrations, drawing people from all over to places like Day Palace or the majestic mountains.

This worship of the Mother Goddess embodies the rebirth, growth, and expansion of our people. It is a religion born out of the specific conditions of our land, enriched by interactions with other spiritual traditions but uniquely ours. The Mother Goddess stands as a symbol of mercy and salvation—both in times of war, when she embodied heroes and warriors, and in times of peace, as she wandered the forests and fields, filling them with song and life.

Her influence runs deep, even into our modern era. The kings of past dynasties recognized her as the most miraculous representation of national creativity, granting her titles like "Queen of the Nation" or "Queen of Magic Harmony." Today, the Mother Goddess continues to inspire millions, embodying the core of our cultural values, independence, and national pride.

As I reflect on our nation's journey, I hope that we are entering a new era of growth and self-esteem, guided by the torch of the Mother Goddess. I dream of writing a book titled *Mother Goddess Worship: The Spirit of My Country.*

I've also made friends with some Jewish people over the years, and I've learned a lot from them. As Einstein said, *"Life is sacred—that is to say, it is the supreme value to which all other values are subordinate."* Judaism, like our native spiritual traditions, emphasizes reverence for life and the moral obligation to serve others.

Yet, there is something else in Jewish tradition—a joy and wonder at the beauty and grandeur of the world that resonates deeply with me. Perhaps my Jewish friend was right when he said that our peoples are like brothers. The only difference is that they worship the Father, while we worship the Mother.

## 15. WHICH SPECK OF DUST WAS TURNED INTO MY BODY...

The Buddha shows us that the Five Skandhas (aggregates)—Rupa (form or matter), Vedana (sensation or feeling), Samjna (thought, cognition or perception), Samskara (formation or mental formation), and Vijnana (consciousness or knowledge)—shape our bodies. Different languages may express them differently, but they all point to the essence of human existence. Together, they form us, with Samjna and Samskara distinguishing our mental aspect.

As the Buddha put it, our body is nothing more than these Five Skandhas. They shape us so intimately that their separation is impossible. Without the mind of comparison (without Samjna), all beings would be the same, but because of Samjna's categorization, we differentiate and give names to things. Thus, we have mountains, rivers, flowers, people, and animals.

The theory of the Five Skandhas is straightforward in the Buddha's teachings, later explained by his disciples in a way that even a distracted mind could grasp. A Buddhist monk once wrote:

· Rupa is like flowers drifting in space, as our bodies appear and disappear like drops of water flowing without direction.

· Vedana is like water bubbles—human happiness and sorrow are just as fleeting.

· Samjna is like the illusion of an oasis a thirsty traveler sees in the desert.

· Samskara is like the outer layer of a banana trunk—too soft to hold anything, whether good or bad.

· Vijnana is like a magic trick—our knowledge changes constantly like a magician's illusion, always finding excuses to explain itself.

The Five Skandhas first appeared in the Buddha's teaching on "Anatman" not long after his Enlightenment. They come together from many unknown factors to form the ego, constantly changing under the laws of Samsara and Cause and Effect.

I've been battling insomnia for years, partly from stress at work and partly because I'm aging faster than I'd like to admit. Sometimes when I come home, I'm greeted

54

by nothing but my dog wagging its tail. No matter how late I go to bed, I have to read a few pages to settle my mind. Sometimes I wake up suddenly, realizing I've left the light on or that I've been dreaming vividly. In those dreams, I often find myself in strange situations—unable to move, trying to cross a busy road, or chatting with an old friend I haven't seen in years.

Then, just as suddenly, I wake up to the real world. I stretch, trying to focus my eyes on the dim morning light outside the window. It's like the call to mindfulness: you wander through life, aimlessly, until something snaps you awake, forcing you to confront reality.

The great poet Rumi once said:

*This being human is a guest house.*

*Every morning, a new arrival.*

*A joy, a depression, a meanness, some momentary awareness comes*

*As an unexpected visitor.*

*Welcome and entertain them all!*

It's been 20 years since I graduated from university and entered this ever-fading life. I've taken countless paths, seen so many new places, and met some kindred souls along the way. I've filled four passports with visa stamps, and I'm now working on my fifth. I remember the early days, traveling around Europe by train. My university was next to a railway station, and the sound of a train horn always startled me.

My first trip to Switzerland in 1990 was a bit of a disaster. I prepared carefully, packing maps and instant noodles that took up half my suitcase. I even brought my Russian rapid water boiler, nicknamed "the submarine," and carried $200 pressed against my chest. But a mistake on the arrival time left me starving on the train for nearly two days. The shame!

When the Berlin Wall fell, and Germany was reunited, I couldn't travel the old route through East Germany. Instead, I took a roundabout journey through Austria, Hungary, and Yugoslavia. As I passed vast green fields and saw nomads with their horses at sunset, I thought, *Maybe I have some nomadic blood after all.*

I've gone through the ups and downs of life, drifting from childhood dreams to harsh realities. And then comes that turning point—a call to mindfulness. We may be pursuing our dreams, but sometimes we end up lost, asking, *Why am I here?*

Waking up from a dream, I often feel caught between the dream world and reality—between vivid memories and fleeting thoughts, between what seems real and what is. There's a version of me I don't fully know—a new version constantly evolving, one that might be my true self, lost in the pursuit of happiness.

In the 1990s, change was everywhere—on every continent, in every country, within every family, and within each of us. After wandering far from home, I returned to start my business. But after a series of ups and downs, I found myself lost again. I spent my days reading and planting trees, hiding from life, unsure where to go next.

One late night, feeling restless, I grabbed my motorbike and rode off into the rain, my bike roaring through the dark. When I returned home at dawn, the rain had stopped, and the buffaloes and cows were beginning their day. Life had reset itself in that small act of rebellion.

For years, I lived in a little house by the river. I spent time in my garden, surrounded by daisies and butterflies. One day, a thought crossed my mind—Zhuangzi's famous dream of being a butterfly. When I woke up, I wondered, *Was I dreaming of being a butterfly, or was the butterfly dreaming of being me?*

There were times when I lost my faith and wondered why I became a trader in the first place. Was it pride? Why had I endured so many highs and lows? Whenever I visited a university, I felt the weight of these questions.

And then, there were moments when I felt completely out of balance—overwhelmed by deadlines, sickness, or just the sheer weight of life. I'd recall those school days when I buried myself in the library, racing to finish my doctorate. When I defended my thesis in 1989, I expected to feel accomplished, but instead, I felt empty. I just wanted to go home.

As life continued with its usual challenges, I realized that when faced with tough decisions, you only have two options: either you find solid ground or you grow wings and fly.

The story goes that a newly ordained monk followed two brothers to the other side of a big lake to meditate. When they arrived, one of the brothers stood up, walked across the lake, and returned to the temple to grab a cushion. The new monk watched, stunned but silent. Later, the other brother stood up, walked across the lake, and fetched a hat.

Inspired, the new monk tried to walk across the lake, but he immediately fell in. He climbed out, tried again, and failed once more. Finally, one of the brothers turned to the other and asked, "Should we show him where the stones are?"

If only someone could show us where the hidden stones in life are—those key moments that lead to success, love, or happiness. We all stumble on the road to power, fame, and fortune, just as we stumble in love. But who can we trust? What path should we take?

Or maybe the answer is that we must trust ourselves.

Life rarely goes the way we plan it. It's full of surprises—some good, some bad. After hiding from life in a house with a tile roof, I moved to an office with a metal roof. I held meetings there during the day and slept there at night. One night, rain dripped onto my face as I slept, a reminder that nothing is ever quite perfect.

Eventually, I took a leadership role at a bank, helping it survive tough times. But after a year, old friends turned their backs on me, and the sincerity of the past faded into hypocrisy. So, I left.

One thing led to another, and I found myself in the real estate business. My friends and I began advising on high-tech parks, hoping to secure prime land. From there, we expanded to other cities and regions, moving like wanderers.

As someone once said, *"When things seem to come to an end, it's time for a new beginning."* And I'd add, *"When things are going well, there's often a deep chasm waiting for us."*

In the world of finance, surprises come quickly—bank stocks that once seemed worthless suddenly skyrocketed. Land prices soared, and I eagerly invested in more banks. But soon, the market flattened, and my hopes dimmed. Still, I reminded myself to be patient.

57

Perhaps I'm still a schoolboy at heart, always in search of something new. Maybe my next journey will take me to Laos, Burma, or Cuba. I don't know what lies ahead, but I'm sure there will be interesting people and places to discover. And teaching others along the way will help me learn more deeply. All I can do is show others where the hidden stones are, helping them avoid the mistakes I've made.

As Tagore once said:

*The same stream of life that runs through my veins*

*Runs through the world and dances in rhythmic measures...*

We wander through life with grand intentions, but in the end, all we want is peace and the chance to be ourselves. The miraculous cycle of life is everywhere—in the tiny cell, in the movement of the Earth and the stars. Our journey begins in our mother's womb and continues in an infinite spiral.

I've read thousands of books and traveled thousands of miles. Now, I stand before the Mother, feeling small yet complete, just as I did at the beginning.

In the end, we find that life isn't a straight highway but a spiral that leads us deeper into our secret selves.

As the Persian poet Rumi wrote, *"My place is a placeless place,"* and it's a shelter where we return to ourselves.

After all, life is a journey—a dance between the Ego and the Self. We may sing songs of impermanence, or we may wake up with joy and mindfulness. But in the end, we all seek that "placeless place" where we find peace, sweetness, and freedom. And, like Tagore, we may discover that:

*I feel that all the stars shine in me.*

*The world breaks into my life like a flood...*

*And the breath of all things plays on my thoughts like a flute.*

It's our choice, but I believe you and I will each find our way to that place.

# 16. THE FANSIPAN JOURNEY

## *Warm-Up*

The idea of conquering **Fansipan Mountain**, the highest peak in my country, was vague to me at first. The name "Fansipan" popped into my head during a work event. Our staff needed a goal, something to look up to, but no one imagined we'd actually go and climb the mountain.

Nearly a year passed, and our routines were in full swing, but that word, "Fansipan," kept echoing in my head. Sometimes I wanted to let it go. Maybe we could plan the trip in October or November. Whenever I saw my colleagues, I'd bring it up, asking them to get ready. Most of the time, I just got polite nods.

Still, I didn't give up. I worked out an itinerary and sent it around, hoping to get some "yeses." Eventually, the date was set, though only a few brave souls signed up. I made some final announcements, threw in some pep talks, and then, to make things tougher, I added a fitness requirement: 50 sit-stands a day or walking 5 kilometers. Secretly, I hoped this would weed out the slackers.

But as the starting date neared, our little group grew to over 20 people—surprisingly large for a bunch of casual trekkers. Everyone seemed excited, and with the event now too big to cancel, I started training myself—standing up and sitting down 100 times a day. My legs stiffened up like iron bars, and I limped around the next day. To my surprise, I learned only a few participants bothered to exercise, which made me think we might have to cancel after all.

Three days before the trip, my assistant and I reviewed the registrations again. The event was still on. I took a deep breath, sent out the final details, and decided to take the plunge.

## *Setting Off*

We left on Friday at noon. Those who stayed behind snapped photos of us like crazy, some even with their belly buttons showing, while others waved with big grins. It felt like the beginning of something great. Our car journey to **Sa Pa** was smooth and nonstop. When we arrived, it was dark. Fog blanketed the town, but the store lights were still glowing, and the streets were alive with people. The vibe was so different—touristy but exciting. It felt great to escape the grind of the city.

After a massive dinner of local dishes, corn, and cassava wine, we headed back to the hotel to prepare for the next day. Things were moving ahead, and what lay ahead in the morning? We had no clue.

We gathered at the hotel lobby at 7 a.m., leaving behind anything we didn't need—though our backpacks still felt way too heavy.

### The 2,200-Meter Peak

Our trek began at **Tram Ton**, at an altitude of 1,800 meters. Our first destination was 2,200 meters. This section of the trail was easy-going, with only gentle slopes. We crossed streams, wandered through forests, and admired the endless mountain views. Stepping around buffalo dung and climbing over fallen trees felt like a true escape from the daily hustle. Hikers in colorful gear and local porters with their heavy loads passed by. The simplicity of it all was refreshing.

As the path flattened, we picked up the pace, weaving beneath branches and heading toward our first campsite. In my haste, I smacked into a tree trunk. Serves me right. Why rush? I should've looked up and taken in the sky, the shifting clouds, and the green ranges stretching before me. Mountains merged with mountains, trees with trees. The wind grew stronger, and the cold started seeping in. I pushed on.

Suddenly, I noticed some purple flowers peeking through the forest, their vibrant petals a reminder of nature's quiet beauty. In the misty twilight, they felt like little gifts of life, quietly blooming amidst the grandeur of the forest. Tagore's words came to mind: "Unmindful I go along the road. Did I not forget the flowers?"

### The 2,800-Meter Peak

After three hours of trekking, we arrived at the 2,200-meter campsite, tired but elated. We lay on canvas sheets under the sky, snacking on steamed rice, sesame salt, and chicken. It felt like a feast in the wilderness.

After a brief rest, we pressed on. The next section was grueling—nothing but rocks and cliffs. We had to use bushes as handholds and even slide down slopes on our butts. There were times I had to jump down a drop and then climb back up with ropes. But as we climbed, the freezing wind whipped through the trees, and clouds hung heavy around us.

*Mountain Night*

We reached the 2,800-meter peak just after 5 p.m. Laughter and chatter filled the air as tents popped up all around. We huddled in the main house, dropping our gear and warming ourselves. Everyone was shivering. After changing into warmer clothes, we collapsed onto the beds, exhausted.

Dinner was a massive spread—stir-fried beef, simmered pork, braised chicken, hot soup, and bottles of rice wine. We even shared some whiskey and sugared ginger to keep warm. It was a feast fit for mountain conquerors.

*Conquering the Summit*

We woke at dawn the next day, fueled by bowls of instant noodles. We quickly geared up, tossed aside any extra weight, and set off before sunrise. Flashlights lit the trail as groups of trekkers zigzagged up the mountain in the dark. Rain drizzled around us, but above was a starry sky and the distant moon.

As the sun began to rise, the landscape came alive. Peaks bathed in golden light, the clouds below us a sea of white. My heart swelled with excitement. We were nearing the top of Indochina.

Finally, after hours of trekking, we saw the summit. The silver pyramid glistened in the sunlight. Cheers erupted from our group. We rushed forward to touch it, overcome with joy. Strangers became instant friends, and we celebrated together.

*Hiking Back Down*

The descent was much lighter—our spirits high from reaching the summit. We retraced our steps, the trail now familiar. Faces that had been strangers at the start of the journey now shared laughter and stories. We snapped photos, exchanged contact info, and made promises to keep in touch.

As we made our way back down, the forest, the mountains, and the bamboo groves seemed to envelop us like old friends. I felt a deep sense of peace, knowing that, for a brief moment, we had conquered something great.

*Farewell*

The next morning, we left **Sa Pa** and headed back home. From the bus window, I watched the lush green mountains and terraced fields roll by. Life is like this—an endless journey. We're all travelers, moving through the vastness of the universe, and every moment is precious.

*(Reaching the summit is a daunting challenge that could make anyone feel discouraged, but the time spent at the top is fleeting compared to the long journey it took to get there. Interestingly, our last night in Sapa felt like a second summit—a place where we lingered longer, soaked in the moment, and truly relished our shared sense of accomplishment and joy.)*

As the poet Basho once said, *"The months and days are the travelers of eternity. The years that come and go are also voyagers."*

See you on the next adventure!

*As I enter the second half of my life, it feels like autumn has arrived, with leaves gently falling around me. I understand now that everything fades—people, events, even the moments we thought would last forever.*

*I've gathered these leaves and captured them on paper. Time, thoughts, and that vague restlessness have drifted away with them. Some of what I've written comes from my own reflections, from the conversations I've had with myself. Other insights have come from friends, family, and even strangers. There were moments when I wanted to express certain truths, but then I hesitated.*

*I've come to realize there's no absolute right or wrong, no clear good or evil. Just fleeting thoughts, unmet desires, and feelings left hanging in the air. Maybe this world has always been made up of those fallen leaves—once vibrant, now gone, yet still part of the cycle. Winter may strip the trees bare, but spring always follows, and life begins anew, with fresh blooms and new growth.*

*People are both competitors and seekers of solitude. We work, create, harvest, and enjoy. If we're fortunate, we do so with a sense of enlightenment and humility, keeping our pride tucked away, where it belongs.*

# PART II

# AUTUMN HAS COME

# 1. HUMANITY, THEN AND NOW

Every time I watch a movie or read a book about the Roman Empire, ancient Indian dynasties, or the Warring States Period in China, I can't help but wonder: Why have people been behaving the same way for over 2,000 years? It's like we're all stuck on repeat—ambition and suffering, conspiracy and calculation, hatred and loss, alliances and betrayals, love and breakups, fortune and revenge, prestige and fraud. It's a timeless playlist.

Dynasties and heroes rise and fall, our understanding of the universe deepens, and the world around us gets decked out with the latest technology. Yet, human behavior? It's like we missed that software update.

Sure, science and technology have worked some wonders. We live longer, can zip around the globe at will, and some folks even take joyrides into space. People are wealthier, surrounded by more gadgets and comforts than ever before. But there's a catch—we're also more stressed, living at hyper-speed, glued to our devices while drifting further away from nature. Society feels more indifferent, almost numb at times. We know more, but we're not any wiser.

It's like we're that student who aces the test but somehow manages to forget the answers in real life. We keep stumbling over the same mistakes, missing the valuable lessons our ancestors left behind. It reminds me of how talented generals throughout history studied the battles of the past and adapted those strategies to win in their own time. Perhaps there's a lesson for us in that too.

So here's the trick to wisdom: Pay attention to the stories of the past. Learn from them. If you can apply that wisdom to your own life, maybe you'll have a shot at navigating this crazy modern world with a little more grace—and maybe even a bit of success.

## 2. REFLECTIONS OF LIFE

### *My Prayer*

My prayer is often simple. I ask the Buddha for a life of harmony:

*Greatness wrapped in simplicity,*

*Power shaped by gentleness,*

*Wisdom gained through continuous learning.*

Yet, the path to achieving this feels overwhelming at times. My life, like many others, is tangled with complexities. Some days, my temper flares, and I struggle to find balance. Despite my deep love for reading and learning, I often find myself starting but rarely finishing—relearning the same lessons over and over.

As I meditated, I pondered how I could be:

*Proud, yet humble;*

*Strong, yet gentle;*

*Talented, yet hardworking.*

Or perhaps:

*Proud, but not distant;*

*Strong, but not harsh;*

*Talented, yet never lazy.*

How can I embody:

*Intimacy, grace, and diligence?*

### *Endurance*

Endurance is essential when life feels unfair. In moments of conflict, when others lose their temper, the key is to stay calm—to resist the urge to meet anger with anger. There is power in quiet composure. When the storm passes, calmness often shifts the tide in our favor.

Life, though, often feels like an endless cycle of emotions—disappointment followed by hope, sorrow followed by joy, and boredom broken by peace. All these emotions spin and churn, endlessly repeating.

Are we simply chasing attachments to the external world, caught up in this whirlwind?

Perhaps true endurance lies in turning inward. Focusing on the breath, recognizing the unity of body and mind, and embracing life's fleeting nature without trying to hold on too tightly.

Endurance, then, becomes a quiet courage—the ability to face life as it is, rather than resisting what cannot be changed.

### Bold Leadership

Bold leadership, much like endurance, requires inner strength. The Buddha embodied compassion, wisdom, and bravery. How can we strive to be more like him, especially during times of chaos and uncertainty? Walking the Eightfold Path is no easy feat, yet in times of crisis, we are called to rise and lead.

History has taught us that while we celebrate democracy and freedom, many civilizations were built not through liberty, but through force. Democracy itself can be a challenge—a delicate balance of uniting millions under one vision, like guiding a ship through stormy seas with everyone rowing in different directions.

Bold leadership is about steering that ship to shore, not with brute strength, but with wisdom, humility, and the ability to build bridges. It's not about wielding power for the sake of power, but about guiding others with compassion and clarity.

### The Cycle of Life

In the end, life offers no definitive right or wrong—only fleeting moments, some fulfilled, some not. These moments drift through time like leaves caught in the wind. And even as they fall, winter does not signify the end. Spring always returns, bringing new growth, fresh leaves, and the beginning of another cycle.

We work, create, reap, and reflect. And if we're fortunate, we find our way with a bit of enlightenment and humility, letting our pride rest quietly in the background as we embrace the unfolding journey ahead.

# 3. NAVIGATING LIFE'S WAVES

## *Human Shaped by Circumstances*

I've often heard stories of extraordinary people—those who somehow overcame the very circumstances that seemed to define them. Whether they were born into difficult situations or faced insurmountable odds, these heroes found a way to not only change their own lives but also shape the lives of others. They transcended adversity and, in doing so, made history.

But here I am, just an ordinary person in a vast, complex society. For most of us, survival depends on the circumstances we're given. We live within the boundaries of our social environments, molded by national politics, our government, and the myriad relationships we have with friends, colleagues, neighbors, and, of course, our families.

The truth is, we're expected to grow and adapt. We're supposed to participate in community activities, join organizations, and contribute to society in meaningful ways. There's no hiding from it. Sometimes, we receive certificates of merit or medals along the way, signs of both our independence and our dependence on the larger world.

Yet, I've seen even the most confident swimmers drown. It's not their lack of talent that gets them, but their overconfidence. They ride the big waves until they're overwhelmed. The survivors? They dive beneath the waves, swallow a few mouthfuls of water, but ultimately, they come out alive.

It's much like the life cycle of a rice plant—sowing, growing, blooming. The flowers of the rice are the result of a long process, nurtured by the soil, water, air, and sunlight. People, like rice plants, are shaped by their circumstances. They grow from what surrounds them. The idea that only extraordinary people can overcome adversity is misleading; the process is what truly matters.

Though we may think of ourselves as separate from our circumstances, we are deeply intertwined with them. They shape us, and we, in turn, shape our futures by how we respond.

*Playing Chess*

One evening, while playing chess with my son, I noticed how quickly my situation on the board shifted from losing to winning. It was a reminder of how life can change in an instant, even when things seem dire.

Before bed, my son asked me, "Is playing chess like doing business?"

I smiled. "Yes," I said, "they're very similar. Chess teaches you strategy—how to assess your position, plan your moves, and deal with your opponent. It shows you that even when you're behind, you shouldn't give up. If you stay calm and focused, you can often turn the game around. It's the same in business. Success often comes down to patience, resilience, and making the best move when the time is right."

Chess, like life, is a game of strategy. It's about adapting to the circumstances in front of you while keeping your end goal in mind. Every move matters, and every situation, no matter how grim, can shift if you approach it with the right mindset.

*

Life, in many ways, is a game we navigate through circumstances beyond our control. Some of us are shaped by adversity, some by privilege, but all of us are influenced by the environments we live in. Whether we're like the swimmers diving under the waves or the chess players trying to outmaneuver an opponent, our strength lies in our ability to adapt, to grow, and to persevere. We are all playing the game, finding our way, one move at a time.

## 4. BOREDOM OF ATTACHMENT

Let's face it, everyday life can be a real snooze-fest. It's like we're all on autopilot, coasting through the same old routine. You wake up, do your thing, rinse, repeat. Some of it becomes so second nature you don't even register it anymore—like nodding to your neighbor or grabbing your coffee mug without looking. Heck, even your house seems indifferent, just standing there, quietly doing its job. The door swings open when you leave for work, shuts behind you when you return, and that's about as much excitement as it gets.

Even your dog, once the epitome of enthusiasm, has downgraded his welcome home routine. No more jumping or slobbery kisses. Now he just gives you that slow tail wag, as if to say, "Oh, you're back? Cool." And if you're lucky, you get a half-hearted glance from your spouse that says, "You again?"

Sometimes, you catch a glimpse of a carefree couple cuddling on the sidewalk, and for a second, you wonder, "Am I missing out on something? Maybe I need a change, a breath of fresh air." But then you remember the drive to work, the same traffic, the same officers in their uniforms trying to direct chaos with flailing arms. You glance at the streets, which seem to wake up just like you—groggily and unenthusiastically. Everything's a bit out of sorts: doors half-open, people half-dressed, some pulling at gates, others preparing their pushcarts like it's just another day. It makes you daydream of a foreign city—cleaner, sleeker, and far more exciting, where life is always changing.

And then you think, "Maybe what I need is a big move, shake things up!" So, you scroll through the internet, maybe check out some real estate listings or dive into the news. The same old stories roll out like clockwork: economic issues, bad debt, corruption, and, of course, the ever-elusive reform. You think, "Is this really all there is?" And suddenly, a distant country pops into your mind. A place where everything's supposed to be better—where the grass is greener, the coffee stronger, and the Wi-Fi faster.

But then, you remember last year's trip. Oh, the thrill of adventure! New places, new faces, that wanderlust burning bright—until homesickness crept in. You started longing for the comfort of your own bed, the same streets, the familiar faces. Traveling was great, but there's something about coming home that just feels... right.

71

And that's when it hits you. The everyday things—the ones you've grown bored of, the routines you've grown tired of—are the very things you love. The people, the streets, even the country that sometimes feels too small for your dreams—they're all part of you. Maybe that's what attachment really is: realizing that the ordinary is extraordinary in its own way, and no matter how far you go, it's these little things that pull you back.

So, go ahead and chase those adventures. Dream of new horizons. But always remember—there's no place quite like home.

## 5. TIME OF DUST

You've probably heard it a million times:

"Time never stops."

"Everything changes with time."

"Time waits for no one."

But let's be honest—daily life has a way of making us forget that. We get caught up in the hustle, whether it's chasing after the next promotion, obsessing over the latest gadget, or just getting lost in the endless scroll of social media. There's arrogance in youth, thinking we've got all the time in the world. And before we know it, days turn into weeks, weeks into months, and suddenly, another year has passed.

Day after day, we go through the motions. Wake up, go to work, come home, repeat. It's easy to fall into the trap of thinking there's always tomorrow. Got something on the to-do list? Eh, it can wait. Why not enjoy a little pleasure now, and worry about the rest later? But time has a funny way of sneaking up on us. One day, we look back and realize how fast it's all gone. The things we put off? They've turned into distant memories. The promises we made? Faded away like old photographs. Even our greatest victories eventually fade into the background, becoming just another piece of history.

Time, as it turns out, is the great equalizer. It smooths out everything—joy, sorrow, success, failure. In the end, our lives are like grains of dust floating in the vast ocean of time.

But here's the kicker: when you really stop and think about how temporary everything is, a little voice inside you whispers, "Make today count." Maybe that's the trick to all this—realizing that even though time can erase just about everything, the choices we make now still matter. They may be small, but they're the seeds of tomorrow's legacy. So don't wait. Make your decisions, take action, and live your life the way you want to, starting today.

Because no one else is going to decide your life for you—not even time.

# 6. ARROGANCE AND ENVY

I've crossed paths with quite a few arrogant folks in my time. You know the type—they've got some genuine talent, sure, but when it comes to social skills, they're about as smooth as sandpaper. They strut around, puffed up with their own self-importance, bragging about the few things they managed to achieve way back when, as if they're recounting tales of saving the world. And of course, they always finish these stories with a dramatic exhale of cigarette smoke right in your face, like some kind of self-appointed philosopher.

Words like *consideration*, *respect*, or *humility* don't even register in their universe. They're so busy looking down from their imagined pedestal, they forget that most of us are too far below for them to even see clearly. It's not that they're above you—it's more like they're just nearsighted.

And heaven help them if they feel like they're slipping into obscurity! They'll jump through hoops to regain the spotlight, desperate to remind the world they still exist. It's as if their very existence depends on staying relevant. Their souls, though? Paper-thin.

Now, if they get a little tipsy, the show gets even better. Suddenly, they're spilling secrets or flashing their prized possessions, trying to prove how important they still are. Word to the wise: stay clear of these types. But if you can't avoid them completely, at least keep a safe distance.

Arrogance and envy are like peanut butter and jelly—always together. Arrogant people can't stand the thought of anyone else being more successful or famous. So, they gather their cronies, whisper venomous gossip about how lucky—but undeserving—everyone else is.

Crowds eat this stuff up. Gossip is practically a spectator sport. And the more people whisper, the bigger the egos grow, and the more that arrogance swells. It's a vicious cycle.

Not too long ago, I ran into one of these characters after a long break. He was practically giddy as he recounted another arrogant guy's downfall. The energy! The enthusiasm! You'd think he was reading the other guy's obituary, savoring every word like it was poetry.

Bingo! Classic case of incurable arrogance. Trust me, keep your distance.

And here's the kicker: it hit me like a ton of bricks that I used to be one of them. I honestly don't know how I managed to look anyone in the eye back then.

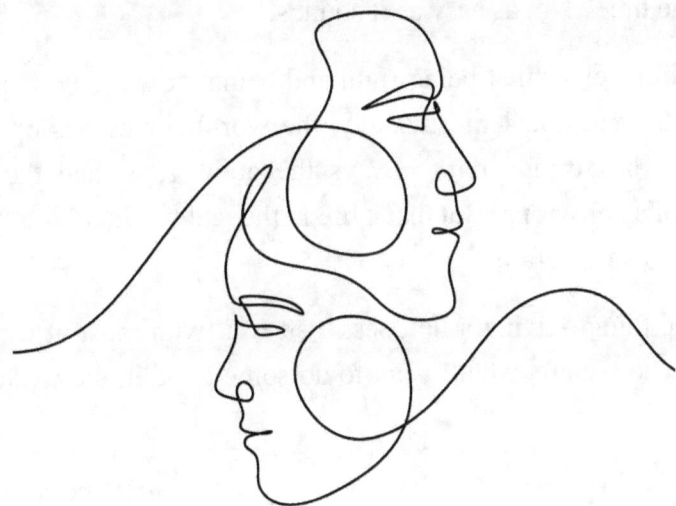

## 7. THE HARD TRUTH

From the time we were kids, we were all told the same thing: "Be honest. Don't lie." Simple enough, right? But as we grow up, it becomes clear that life isn't so black and white. Good and evil, right and wrong—they're often just a matter of perspective, shaped by who's looking and what they stand to gain.

Inside each of us, there's a mix of good and bad. One moment, we do something we're proud of; the next, we make a choice that's… well, less than ideal. And the line between the two? It's often blurrier than we'd like to admit. What's considered 'good' or 'bad' can shift depending on whose shoes you're standing in. That's just how life works.

That's also why living with the truth can feel like trying to balance on a tightrope. You're expected to be truthful by society's standards, but here's the catch: telling the truth *all* the time? Not as easy as it sounds.

We like to tell ourselves that being right and being strong are one and the same. Spoiler alert: they're not. Unfortunately, the world sometimes operates on this flawed belief. The strong aren't always the good guys, and the weak aren't necessarily foolish or wrong. But that's life in the real world. If you don't have the strength (yet), tread carefully.

Still, here's the thing—living a lie doesn't sit well with most of us. Deep down, regardless of who we are, we all want to do some good in the world, even if it's just a little.

So, what's the best approach? Be honest with yourself first and foremost. It's the only friendship that really counts in the end. And if honesty seems too much for the moment, there's always the option to stay silent. That's still better than a lie.

Here's the upside: the strong who thrive on lies will eventually hit the floor. It might take a while, but it happens. And in the meantime, if there's something small and good you can do for someone having a rough time, go ahead and do it. No act of kindness, no matter how tiny, is wasted.

## 8. LESSONS IN LETTING GO

### *Going with the Flow*

Sitting in a Zen temple, reflecting on the past twenty years of life's ups and downs, I had this thought: after all the back-and-forth, some things have worked out, others... not so much. Maybe it's time to just let things be.

Old tasks will eventually get done. New opportunities will arise. The company will grow at its own pace.

Lao Tzu once said that the Tao is about "succeeding without doing anything." I've often wondered if that's true. Is letting go the secret to moving forward?

### *Finding Peace*

The trick, I've learned, is to find peace in the present moment. Mindfulness helps with that, especially with three key reminders:

1. The present moment is the most important.

2. The people you meet right now are the most important.

3. Bringing peace and happiness to them—and to yourself—is the most important.

That's when true peace shows up in your life and your work.

### *Want vs. Like*

Here's a little insight I've stumbled upon: Want and Like—two words we often confuse for each other—are actually very different.

"Want" is driven by logic, necessity, or habit. You want what everyone else seems to want. "Like," though, comes from a different place—your emotions, your personality, your own quirks.

Sometimes, what you want and what you like are not the same. And if you're willing to let go of some of those "wants," you free yourself up to focus on what you truly like.

So, think twice before you chase after something. It's worth deciding whether it's something you really want... or something you simply like.

And maybe, just maybe, by letting go, you'll get exactly where you need to be.

# 9. LEGACY AND FREEDOM

## *Your Own Legacy*

I've been traveling the North and South for years. One day, waking up with a long face, I was struck by life's impermanence. It's a constant cycle of building, destroying, and building again. Countless houses have been erected and then torn down; countless families have risen and fallen over the years. Time leaves its mark on old, mossy structures. So, why do we strive to build something big and pass it on to the next generation? Does that really last? Does it even work?

Companies come and go. They may stand for 30, 50, or even 100 years, but eventually, they slip into oblivion. Business owners—once celebrated—fade from memory. Where have they all gone?

Looking back at our history, we see dynasties rise and fall in my country. Nothing seems to last very long. War after war, and very little remains beyond 100 years—maybe a few old graves, temples, or pagodas. Even they become little more than moss-covered ruins.

So, what's the point in fooling ourselves with the illusion of creating something big for future generations? The real value lies in doing something meaningful for ourselves and others right now—not for some far-off future.

## *A Free Soul*

Life ties us up in all kinds of knots—family obligations, social commitments—it's like we're constantly tethered to something. We aren't really free.

Every language has its own way of expressing ownership: my money, my health, my house, my spouse, my kids, my country, my city, my hometown. All these "my" attachments hold us down.

But those attachments don't stop outside forces from threatening to take away what we value. Your possessions could be lost, your loved ones could be separated from you, or your very freedom could be taken away. And don't forget the invisible forces—like tiny bacteria—that can steal your health or even your life.

Life is fragile. Have you ever watched an army of ants scurrying for food or gazed out of a plane window at the endless lines of people and traffic? It makes you wonder—are we really any different from those ants?

But here's the twist: no matter how strong those external forces may be, they can never control your soul. Your soul is free—it belongs to the Universe.

While your life may be short and bound by limitations, your soul is infinite. And if you live with integrity and dignity, no force can truly defeat you. Even if you're oppressed or stripped of your freedom, your soul remains untouchable.

So, let your soul soar free—with dignity, no matter the circumstances.

## 10. DEDICATION AND ORDER

God created humans to be almost perfect, didn't He? We've got a heart, a mind, a body, and all the essential parts to go about our business. We can think, work, create, love, hate, fight, search, gather, and play—all while daydreaming about what else we could be doing.

It's funny, though. With all these capabilities, we often fall into the trap of thinking we can do it all at once. Maybe that's why God gave us two brain hemispheres, two arms, and two legs. It's as if He set us up for the ultimate challenge: juggling as many things as we possibly can, all while holding onto our persistence, bravery, and passion for what we truly want in life.

But here's the catch: you can't succeed if you don't dedicate yourself fully. God might've blessed us with pairs of almost everything, but we only get one heart. And success? Well, that demands all your love, energy, time, and focus.

As brilliant as we are—capable of creating art, solving math, and memorizing an overwhelming amount of information—our brains work best in sequence, not all at once. You can't count up from 1 to 10 while counting down from 10 to 1 at the same time. And trying to draw a circle with one hand while drawing a square with the other? Good luck with that.

The truth is, we might be able to do just about anything, but we're designed to do it one step at a time. Success requires patience, passion, and doing things in order. That's just the way God planned it.

I only wish I'd figured this out a bit earlier. At nearly 50, I've realized some things just can't be undone. But hey, I'm still lucky—I've got one heart, and it's got plenty of miles left in it.

## 11. CAREFREE FRIENDSHIP

Every relationship involves some form of exchange—whether it's now or in the future. It doesn't matter if it's between colleagues, friends, lovers, parents and kids, or even within a religion. At some point, there's a give and take.

Take love, for instance. At first, it's all affection and intimacy—everything feels like a romantic high. But, let's be honest, that doesn't last forever. Love can fade, or it morphs into a mix of favor and responsibility.

Parent-child love is precious, no doubt. But in many ways, it's a one-way street that often leaves parents feeling a little lonely as their kids grow up and move on with their own lives. Religion can feel one-sided, too, with its devotion and faith flowing in a single direction.

And then there's the world of colleagues, classmates, and mentors. These relationships evolve based on circumstances. Sometimes, they grow stronger and become sources of support, and other times, they fizzle into half-hearted pleasantries and polite nods. You never know.

Men come to women seeking solace, both physically and emotionally. Let's face it, men can be a little lonely and a bit arrogant—they want someone to pamper them. Women, on the other hand, are like climbing vines—delicate, soft, and in need of a strong wall to lean on. They want support, strength, and, ultimately, possession of a man's heart.

So, when it comes down to it, love is often a deep exchange. In flowery language, it sounds sacred and beautiful. But strip it down, and it's a give-and-take.

Now, friendship? That's a different beast. A true friendship—especially between two men—can be wonderfully carefree.

When it's real, it's not about what one can get from the other. It's not selfish or opportunistic. It doesn't matter if they're next door or thousands of miles apart; they understand each other without needing to say a word. They reflect each other's strengths and flaws, knowing one another like they know themselves.

It's like being two rough, lonely islands in the vast ocean of life. These friends weather the storms, supporting each other quietly, like soil absorbing rainwater. There's no pretense, just an unspoken bond of care and respect.

That's a rare thing—a truly carefree friendship. And let's be honest, finding such a friend is like striking gold. If you've got one or two of those in a lifetime, consider yourself blessed.

## 12. A FREE SOUL

Your life is tangled up in family ties, social obligations, and the occasional nosy neighbor. Freedom? Well, let's just say it's on a tight leash.

Every language has a way of marking territory: my money, my health, my house, my spouse, my kids, my country, my town. Mine, mine, mine—so much "mine" that you start feeling like you're running a museum of attachments.

That's why you're not exactly free.

We spend so much time holding on to things. But here's the kicker: some unseen force—whether it's a financial crisis, a relative's bad decision, or even a sneeze in the wrong place—could strip away everything you hold dear. Not to mention that a rogue bacteria could lay you out faster than you can say "organic."

Fragile, right? Life's funny like that. You ever watch ants scurrying around, each one busy with their tiny tasks? Ever glance out of an airplane window and realize people look like ants too, hustling and bustling in their little lines? Sometimes we're not much different—ants with credit cards.

But here's the twist: no matter how many external forces knock you around, they can't touch your soul. That's yours, and it belongs to something way bigger than traffic jams and tax returns.

Sure, your time here might be limited, but your soul? Infinite. Boundless. And if you live with integrity and dignity, you're untouchable in the ways that matter.

Even if life's circumstances try to box you in or take your freedom, your soul stays wild and free—like a kite that breaks loose from its string and dances with the wind.

So, go ahead. Let your soul roam free, with all the dignity of a lion on a coffee break.

## 13. EMOTIONAL LOVE

I've seen love in all its technicolor glory—passion, happiness, suffering, anger, betrayal, jealousy, loneliness, despair, and, yes, even hatred. The sweet moments? Oh, they're like candy—gone too fast, leaving you with long stretches of worry and regret.

People write all these beautiful verses, sing all those swoon-worthy songs about love, but let's be real: that bliss? Temporary. It's just a brief vacation from reality before it turns around and bites you. Never forget, when you're making love with your partner, you're also cozying up to your future nemesis. Sounds harsh, but it's true. That affection you're feeling? It has a funny way of igniting the fires of selfishness, shamelessness, and a touch of arrogance.

We like to think we've "won" when we fall in love, like we've somehow captured the prize. But honestly, love has its own ideas about who's in charge. One minute you're on top of the world, the next, you're tied up in emotional knots, more captive than conqueror. Pain and suffering are practically love's sidekicks—they show up when you least expect it. And trust me, they never miss a date night.

So, yes, love is a battlefield (thanks, Pat Benatar). But it's not about winning or losing; it's more like a never-ending chess match, where the target is each other's well-being. In love, you're going to get hurt. That's just part of the deal. Making love? Well, that's the truce before the next skirmish.

Here's the catch, though: you can't stay on guard forever in love. If you did, you'd stop loving. And just like that—no more fight, no more love. So maybe love isn't just a battle after all; maybe it's more like a roller coaster you can't get off of. You scream, you laugh, you cry, and then—against all logic—you get back in line for another ride.

## 14. THE WISDOM PUZZLE

By the time Confucius hit 40, he claimed the world no longer baffled him—he had seen enough to get the gist of it all. And honestly, after four decades, most of us can relate. Life starts playing on a loop: joy, sadness, success, failure, health, illness, birth, death. The reruns keep coming. It's not that we can predict everything, but we've gotten pretty good at anticipating the general storyline. Yet, even with all that experience, life has a way of humbling us. There's always something new just beyond our line of sight.

This is where the real challenge lies—navigating the familiar landscape of our own experiences without getting caught in the traps we should have seen coming. Wisdom is knowing better, but it doesn't always mean doing better. Every now and then, we still manage to stumble, usually when we're too full of ourselves to hear the warnings from our own inner compass.

And that's the tricky part, isn't it? You can be brilliant, successful, and wise, but if you let arrogance creep in, that wisdom starts slipping through your fingers. We've all seen it—people who seem to have it all figured out, only to crash when they reach their 50s or 60s. Why? Because they stop listening—to themselves, to the world, to what life is trying to whisper in their ear.

Life, and business too, is like a giant puzzle. It doesn't really take shape until all the interactive pieces come into play—people, opportunities, moments. At first, nothing fits; the pieces seem random, the struggle endless. But that's part of the thrill. You wrestle with it, test different combinations, fail, try again. And then, just when you're ready to walk away, frustrated and exhausted, everything clicks. The puzzle pieces snap into place, and the way forward is suddenly clear. That's the sweet spot, the moment of revelation. But of course, it's just a brief pause before the next puzzle begins.

The key is this: stay humble, stay curious, and keep listening. Wisdom may come with age, but it doesn't mean the game ever gets easier. You just get a little better at solving the puzzles along the way.

# 15. WISE OR FOOLISH, BE ALIVE IN THE NOW

Maybe Chuang Tzu was the first to point it out: if you're wiser than everyone around you, don't be shocked if they start resenting you. It's funny how wisdom has a way of turning people off when it makes them feel inadequate. Too much arrogance and suddenly, you're not the wise sage—you're the thorn everyone's ready to pluck out.

But then there are the fools. The ones who charge ahead, taking on things way beyond their reach. They're often the ones who get knocked down the hardest. And let's face it, people love following the strong horse, not the one chasing its tail.

To survive in this big social game, you have to know when to play it cool and when to step on the gas. It's a delicate dance—sometimes you go forward, sometimes you retreat. And, like it or not, you have to adjust your pace based on what's happening around you.

Here's the twist: nobody's so wise that they win it all, and nobody's so foolish that they lose it all. Life has a funny way of balancing the scales. The real trick? Learning how to adapt. It's in those adjustments that we start to grasp what this whole ride is about. Just don't get too confident too quickly—life's got a habit of humbling those who think they've got it all figured out.

Whether you're the smartest person in the room or blissfully clueless, one thing's for sure: we all end up in the same place. Disease, old age, and, eventually, a nice plot of land six feet under. Morbid, sure, but oddly grounding. As time goes on, we get better at navigating the world, learning how to fit in, trying to score more successes, acquire more stuff, and chase our dreams.

It's the classic human story, and we have to admire the effort. But there's something so wonderfully desperate about it all, isn't there?

So, here's the best approach: Be wise—but not too wise. Throw in a little foolishness for good measure. Be brave—but keep a touch of caution in your back pocket. Be faithful—but don't be afraid to play a few tricks when you need to. Stay dynamic, but don't rush too fast. Be profound, but don't be afraid to keep things light sometimes.

In the end, it's all about balance—just like seasoning your food. A little salt is good, even if it's just vegetarian.

## 16. GRACELESS AND INNOCENT

I've met plenty of people who are, well, graceless. Not that they're ugly—some of them are quite attractive, actually. And it's not about a lack of brains, either; some of these folks are smart enough to paper their walls with diplomas. But there's something missing. They walk through life with the same indifference you'd expect from a houseplant.

Sure, they'll laugh out loud at some random thing that tickles their fancy, but the humor? It's the kind that leaves you scratching your head, wondering what joke you missed. They ask spontaneous questions like wide-eyed children, seemingly eager to understand the world. But here's the catch—they don't care about the answers. Nope, they just need to get those thoughts out, like a soda bottle that's been shaken one too many times. Pop the cap, and there they go.

They've got their quirks, too. Maybe it's in their clothes, or how they apply makeup. Sometimes it's like they've taken fashion tips from a funhouse mirror—nothing seems to fit quite right, yet somehow, it's all part of their innocent charm. They parade through life with this odd mix of naivety and cluelessness, and you can't help but wonder if they know something the rest of us don't—or if they're just winging it with a kind of reckless, innocent abandon.

Innocent or not, graceless or charming, they move through life like a breeze that occasionally knocks over a vase. You can't always explain why they're the way they are, but somehow, their presence—awkward and all—adds something to the room. And maybe, just maybe, there's a certain grace in that after all.

## 17. PATIENT MEANS PROACTIVE

All suffering in life stems from dissatisfaction: not getting what you want, losing someone you love, feeling like a failure, betrayal by friends, defeat by enemies, poor health, or even an unsatisfactory sex life. It's the gap between what we desire and what we experience that fuels our discontent.

Worry? It's like an uninvited guest—always tagging along wherever you go, no matter what you're doing. It's something we have to learn to live with because, like it or not, it's part of the human condition. There's no escape from it.

But here's where patience comes in as your strongest ally. When you patiently accept what you can't change, you find a way to rise above it. Waiting through your troubles without giving in to despair? That's perseverance.

When you take a step back and let go of your need to control every outcome, that's humility in action. And practicing patience day by day, taking small, steady steps forward—that's persistence. Choosing to forgive when you'd rather hold on to a grudge? That's grace. Loving and serving others even when it's hard? That's real love. Listening deeply and striving to understand? That's empathy.

It takes courage to be patient. It's not passive; it's an active choice. And perseverance will carry you through the long journey toward whatever destination you have in mind. Success? It's fleeting, always changing, so it's the journey itself that truly matters. There are no shortcuts, no quick fixes. Patience is the fuel that keeps you moving forward.

And when it comes to the end of that journey—death—patience will comfort your soul. It allows you to face the inevitable with peace instead of fear.

Being patient with life's challenges is the smartest thing you can do. It's the ultimate challenge, but also the greatest gift.

Patience brings peace. With it, worry loses its grip, and your soul finds calm. Strength and wisdom follow. In the end, patience is the most proactive thing you can practice—it's not just waiting; it's actively creating the space for peace and strength to grow within you.

## 18. YOU NEED YOUR ENEMY

Enemies. They're all around you, whether you notice them or not. Sometimes they show up right in your face; other times, they're lurking in the shadows, plotting from a distance. They can be anyone—an old friend, a relative, or even some random person you've never met. One day, out of nowhere, they step onto the scene as your enemy.

The funny thing is, your enemy often appears when you've got something you want—a goal, a viewpoint, a need. It's as if the universe says, "Oh, you want that? Here's someone who wants it too. Let the games begin." They push you, drive you to the edge, making you think harder, work smarter, strive longer. They're the perfect motivators—whether you like it or not.

Your direct enemy? They teach you how to attack, to fight head-on. That old friend who suddenly turns into an enemy? They're sharpening your defense skills. And that person who follows the crowd, stirring the pot? They remind you of the conspiracies lurking beneath the surface. Each one, in their own annoying way, is helping you level up. And as much as it stings, you'll learn a bit of humility along the way.

If your enemy happens to be a group of people, congratulations—you're about to learn the art of building and leading an army. Life's a battlefield, and sometimes you win, sometimes you lose. But during those moments of truce, take a step back. Understand your enemy. They might just be teaching you more than you think.

One thing's for sure: you've got to win the final battle, or at least fight to a draw. Whatever you do, don't throw in the towel. Don't give up, don't run away. Because here's the twist: when you're tired and ready to wash your hands of it all, when you wish for a life with no more competition, no more enemies—guess what? The most dangerous enemy is still waiting for you. And that enemy? It's you.

The battle with yourself is the toughest one. It's long, it's painful, and it lasts until the end. But here's the kicker: you can't live without your enemies. They're part of the package. So, you might as well accept it.

## 19. THANK YOU

Thank you for being my wife. For teaching me those first lessons in love and suffering. For sharing warm dinners, a cozy bed, and the stories that made us laugh and think. Thank you for giving me moments of patience, understanding, and space when I needed it.

Thank you to the second, the fifth, the thousandth woman who crossed my path— each leaving behind a smile, a tender glance, love, and a touch of compassion and grace. Thank you to the one with soft skin and thick black hair that rests on my chest at night, who gives me all her love and trust.

Thank you for the wonderful children who remind me of my own childhood as I watch them grow up before my eyes. Thank you for staying close to my family, for bringing joy to my parents when I couldn't be there, and for being there when I found it hard to express my own love to them.

Thank you for helping me see my own weaknesses—my quick temper, my superficiality, my tendency to get caught up in the busyness of life. Thank you for your strength and patience in facing the sorrows I've caused, even when I didn't mean to. Thank you for being gentle yet quiet, forgiving but sometimes distant. You've made me fall deeper in love with you in ways I never expected.

Thank you for giving so much while getting so little in return. Thank you for showing me what loneliness feels like, so I can truly appreciate what love means and value the relationships that matter most.

Thank you for being the good in my life—the warm bread, the sweet honey, the strong wine, the salt that adds flavor to everything.

Thank you, women.

## 20. THE POWER OF DISCRETION

Flowery words and grand gestures have a funny way of setting us up for disappointment. You paint the picture too pretty, and eventually, when reality shows up, it can't compete with the fantasy. It's like building a house out of air—you've got the shape, but nothing solid to stand on. In Asia, there's often a tension between appearance and reality—people may present one thing but be something entirely different beneath the surface. So, what's the solution? Be discreet and humble. After all, talent shines brighter when it's not competing with an ego.

Speaking of talent, I once knew a guy for 20 years—a real sharp one, full of potential—and yet, he went bankrupt. It felt like watching a tragedy in slow motion, the kind where you know how it's going to end but can't look away. Life, when you boil it down, is surprisingly simple. It's about taking what's plentiful and delivering it to where it's scarce. Talent is best when paired with modesty. Giving and receiving, wealth and restraint, ambition and a bit of secrecy—all of it needs balance.

Our ancestors knew this. They warned us about it, even if we don't always listen. The problem is, people don't stop when they should. They forget about limits, chasing more even when enough would have been just fine. But losing? It's not the end of the world. If you've got real talent, stay patient. Your moment will come—if you don't rush it.

And remember, the wise are smart enough to learn from other people's mistakes. Why reinvent the wheel of failure when someone else has already rolled it for you?

Life's Little Paradoxes

Some paradoxes you might find familiar:

- *The faster you move, the later you arrive.*

- *A big reputation often hides behind a scandal.*

- *Those who are discreet go far; those who brag burn out fast.*

- *The higher the position, the less valuable the words.*

- *Love that thrives often suffers the weight of indifferent benefits.*

- *Huge careers? They usually start with small steps.*

## 21. WISDOM AND THE TEACHER

From the moment we're kids, we're taught that the goal is to get smarter. School lessons fill our heads with facts about the world, and exams do their best to separate the so-called "smart" ones from the rest of the pack.

Then comes graduation, and we're thrown into the wild unknown called life. It's full of surprises, a few disasters, and a lot less reading than we promised ourselves we'd do. Instead of textbooks, life itself starts teaching us through trial and error—mostly error. We stumble, we fall, we get back up, and somehow, we come out a little wiser for it. Experience turns out to be the best classroom, though the tuition can be pretty steep.

Eventually, we all start to make sense of the world in our own way. We develop a personal system of concepts and beliefs, built from what we've learned, lived, and maybe even survived. And maybe that's what intelligence really is—the ability to create your own playbook for life based on everything you've picked up along the way.

But here's the kicker: a truly wise person is someone who never stops learning—both from life and from books. It's like climbing a mountain; the higher you go, the more you can see both the path behind you and the one still ahead. That perspective is golden, which is why someone who's been around longer or who's really good at their craft often becomes a great teacher.

Still, life has its own way of throwing curveballs. As the saying goes, desperate diseases require desperate remedies. And sometimes, life hands you a challenge that no textbook could have prepared you for. That's when you realize that learning isn't just about finding one great teacher—it's about having many teachers along the way. But if you're bold enough, you'll discover something deeper: your worst enemy is yourself, and sometimes, the greatest teacher is that enemy staring back at you.

## 22. LOVE YOURSELF - LOVE THE NATION

What does the nation mean to you?

One morning, I woke up to the familiar, slightly robotic sound of a loudspeaker echoing in the distance. I tried to tune in, but whatever it was saying just floated past me like white noise. So, I let it go. A new day was starting. Soon, the streets would be flooded with people and vehicles, all in a hurry—rushing here, waiting there, and always moving back and forth like some chaotic dance we all know by heart.

As usual, I'd head off to the office or somewhere—doing something that felt necessary, even if it was hard to pin down exactly why. Life can be funny that way: full of vague tasks that somehow feel essential, so you just carry on with them like clockwork.

Then suddenly, a sharp motorbike horn blared nearby, and my thoughts scattered. I found myself remembering places I've visited, the times I struggled in foreign cities, lost among unfamiliar faces. My mind drifted to those ever-green forests, the endless, deserted roads, winding mountain passes towering over the ocean, and sandy beaches baking under the midday sun. And when night fell, I'd watch the ocean transform into a sparkling sky of squid boats casting their beams, like stars brought down to earth.

My memory then shifted to roads being paved, bulldozers and steamrollers grinding away, and villages lined with temporary metal-roofed houses that looked as if they were holding on by sheer willpower. A new day, full of its own grit and hardship.

The loudspeaker's voice finally cut off, replaced by a familiar tune that I couldn't quite place. I found myself wanting to sing along. Funny how music can do that— feel both familiar and strange at the same time.

And that's when it hit me: The nation isn't just flags and borders. It's everything around you, everything close to you. It's all the days you've lived, the places you've seen, and the people you've met. The mountains and hills? They're your flesh and blood. The scenery is tied to your emotions. The river flows with your thoughts, and the ocean? That's your restlessness. All of it together forms your soul and body. The nation is inside you. You *are* the nation.

We're tied to the nation not because of duty, but because we're made of the same stuff. When you love yourself, when you live for yourself, you're already serving the nation in ways that run deeper than any anthem. So, wake up. A new day is here, and it's yours to live.

## 23. KNOWLEDGE AND WISDOM

I've spent a lot of time in universities and libraries, and I have to admit, there's nothing quite like the thrill of buying a new book. Even back when finances were tight, I still found myself sneaking into bookstores to read a few pages, getting that fix from the smell of fresh ink on crisp paper like a book addict in denial. And when I didn't know what else to do, I'd turn to an old storybook for comfort, rereading it like it held some hidden secret I'd missed the first time around. I read whenever I can—on the way to work, during meeting breaks, even in the bathroom, before bed, or sometimes right before...well, you know, life's other pleasures.

But here's the truth: I haven't even finished 2/3 of the books I own. Some of them I've only skimmed the preface. Others, I've read halfway through and walked away with barely a nugget of wisdom. Some books went completely over my head.

And yet, when you step into a national library or one of those sprawling international ones with endless shelves, it's easy to feel small. Overwhelmed, even. Don't even get me started on the Internet—just one click, and you're drowning in an ocean of knowledge.

So here's the kicker: if anyone thinks they're truly knowledgeable, they're probably just fooling themselves. Knowledge is limitless—much like the depths of our consciousness. The more you think you know, the more you realize how little you've grasped.

How do you avoid getting lost in that vast ocean of information?

In my experience, there are two methods that actually work.

The first: Focus. Pick one field and go all in. Read everything you can, think deeply, and match what you've learned with real-life experiences. Keep at it, and eventually, you'll hit the peak of that field. And once you're standing there, you'll notice that from the top of one mountain, you can see the patterns in all the others. Sure, the peaks may be different, but you start to recognize the common threads tying them together. That's when wisdom starts kicking in.

The second method? Stop all the reading and intellectual scavenger hunts. Instead, read your own life. Experience it, reflect on it. Clear your mind—let it become as

95

still as a mountain lake. Slowly, you'll begin to see through the clutter. Your mind sharpens, becoming clearer and clearer over time. And before you know it, you'll start to understand the world in ways no book could ever teach you. It turns out, the real lessons come from living, not from absorbing endless facts.

That's when you realize—you've become wise. You've awakened to something bigger.

## 24. PAINFUL INDIFFERENCE

It's tough to stay grounded in this chaotic life. What we see and what we hear often don't match up with reality. We're caught between moments of bravery and cowardice, real friendships and flashy lies. Our self-esteem constantly takes hits, learning lessons from actions that leave us cringing with regret. And let's not forget the endless parade of stupid decisions and evil schemes that seem determined to trip us up.

The city comes alive at dusk, bathed in lights, with traffic jammed in every direction, car horns blaring as if the noise itself could push the line forward. Somewhere on a street corner, loud music competes with the chaos, creating a kind of urban symphony. Meanwhile, far from the city, villages sit quietly in darkness, only disturbed by the faint crackle of a radio or TV coming from a house with a slanted tile roof. It's like the world is spinning two different versions of itself: one fast-paced and neon-lit, the other slow and drenched in shadows.

We love to talk about progress—factories springing up, industrial parks multiplying, new cities popping up like mushrooms after the rain. But out in those villages, not much has changed in a thousand years. As you stroll down these so-called "civilized" streets, what do you really see? Ugly houses of all shapes and sizes thrown together, some clinging to office buildings or tucked against old villas like afterthoughts. It's like a game of architectural Tetris gone horribly wrong. And then there's that dusty old garbage truck, creaking down the road, spewing out exhaust and rattling like it's held together by duct tape and hope, collecting trash with a fanfare that's hard to ignore.

And amidst all this progress and noise, we somehow manage to overlook the quiet desperation around us. Look closely enough, and you'll see the homeless huddled in doorways, covered in whatever scraps of warmth they can find, invisible to the world rushing past them. You see addicts lingering on street corners, eyes glazed, waiting for their next escape. They've become part of the scenery—blending in with the urban mess, just another problem people don't have time to solve.

Everyone's in a hurry, rushing through life, worrying about things both real and imagined. They move quickly, heads down, too busy to stop for much of anything. Sure, they feel a flicker of sympathy when they hear about something sad—whether it's a news story or a glimpse of someone less fortunate—but it fades as quickly as it came. The thought crosses their mind, "I'm just a speck of dust in this vast universe. What can I really do?" And so they carry on, saying nothing.

The radio crackles with more news—floods in the central region. People are losing their homes, kids can't go to school. Tomorrow, when I head to work, I'll probably toss in some old clothes and a little of my paycheck to help the cause. But for now? I'll just let it sit there in the back of my mind, one more tragedy in a world full of them.

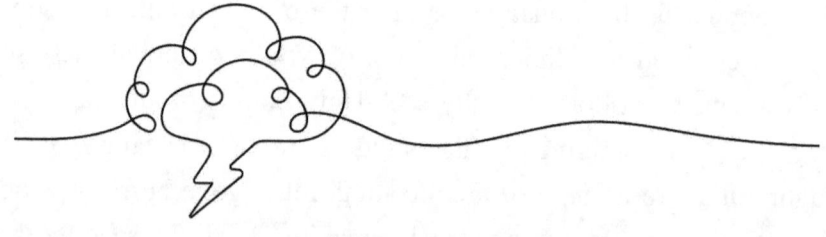

## 25. LIFE'S LITTLE IRONIES

**Fame**

Tough economic times have a way of revealing something interesting: the truly resourceful businessmen are nowhere to be found. It's like they've gone into hiding, while the wealthy and famous folks you see splashed across the media? Well, they're mostly just making noise. Empty vessels with a lot of airtime.

Ever notice how many big-shot CEOs go bankrupt overnight? One minute they're riding high, the next they're face-planting for the whole world to see. And yet, somehow, we're all entertained by their spectacular fall from grace. It's as if their fame was just a setup for the punchline.

**Artisans**

Here's a story for you: a master butcher uses the same knife for 19 years. Bad butchers hack away at the meat and are constantly replacing their tools. The good ones? They're careful, changing their knife only once a year. But the skilled ones—the real artisans—they know exactly how to separate the meat from the bone without a scratch. Their knife stays sharp for nearly two decades.

What's the lesson here? It's unpredictable when someone reaches true mastery in their craft. But whatever the field, the key is to be flexible. Because in life, even the most skilled artisan knows when to adapt—or risk becoming just another hack with a blunt blade.

**Fear**

Time flies, doesn't it? You're always busy, always on the move, chasing the next thing on your to-do list. And somehow, in all that rushing, you forget to pay attention to the one thing that matters most—you.

Then, one day, it hits you. Maybe it's a sharp pain in your chest, trouble catching your breath, or a random ache that sneaks up on you in the shower. It's just a feeling, but it rattles you. Fear creeps in, and suddenly, the thought of old age—of time slipping through your fingers—grabs hold. For a moment, you regret all those wasted hours and misplaced priorities.

But don't worry—that regret won't stick around too long. After all, tomorrow's worries are waiting to sweep you right back into the whirlwind of daily life.

# 26. CONSCIENCE IS THE HIGHEST COURT

Everything you do in life will eventually slip away—love, hatred, joy, anxiety, success, failure, sincerity, lies—it all fades with time. Old age and daily worries have a way of scrubbing your memory clean. Even the moments where you felt deeply connected to someone or burdened by responsibilities toward family and society—they don't stick around forever. Compliments or criticism, fame or shame, whether for you or someone else? They're like yesterday's newspaper. You glance at it, maybe skim a headline or two, and then toss it aside without a second thought. It's all just external noise—like the weather, dust, or even life's bigger storms. They blow through, and then they're gone, never to be heard from again.

But there's one thing that never leaves you alone: that sneaky little voice in your head. It's always there, asking questions, dishing out critiques, sometimes being way too complimentary, and other times being downright harsh. This inner voice is your conscience, and it's got more staying power than a bad commercial jingle. It will follow you all the way to your grave, whispering in your ear about what's right and wrong, what's true and false. Your conscience is like a relentless prosecutor, digging into every thought, action, and intention. Sometimes, it's cruel enough to tear you apart mentally, and other times, it's the only thing that offers you comfort, praise, or even a solid defense.

The kicker is that what your conscience does to you depends entirely on what you're up to—whether you're being a decent human being or quietly plotting your next questionable move.

So, in the grand scheme of things, your conscience is the scariest court you'll ever face. Everything else—the fleeting moments, the noise, the drama—will fly away like dust in the wind. But that inner voice? It never lets you off the hook.

## 27. LIVE IN THE NOW

I've read more books on meditation and Buddhism than I can count, and I've spent years pondering the meaning of life. Every one of those teachings has something to say about living in the now and appreciating what you have in the present moment. Sounds great, right? But let's be honest—it's a lot easier said than done.

We're all guilty of chasing whatever is in front of us—whether it's success, money, or just the next thing on our to-do list. And the question is, does all that chasing bring us peace? Spoiler alert: probably not.

Oddly enough, the rare times we do fully live in the moment often come during the most intimate of moments. Let's talk about sex for a second—when you're with someone and both of you are completely present, that's when you realize that nothing else matters. The only thing that exists is the person in front of you, and the most important thing is the connection you're sharing. When that moment hits, you've nailed it—literally and figuratively. It's pure, undistracted presence, and that's why it feels so powerful.

If we approached everything with that same level of presence—whether we're working, eating, or having a conversation—we might just unlock the secret to living life to the fullest. It's possibly the essence of Zen, Buddhism, and, well, the art of not letting life pass you by.

So, maybe living in the now isn't just about meditating on a mountaintop. Maybe it's about bringing that same focus and appreciation to the everyday moments—because when you do, life suddenly gets a lot more meaningful. And fun.

## 28. COUNT ON YOURSELF

I've been through a few crises—okay, maybe more than a few—and there's one thing I've learned: when things go south, don't count on help from the outside. Seriously, no one's coming to the rescue. Not your family, not your friends, not even that one person you once helped out of a jam. Everyone's got their own stuff going on, and they're not about to drop it for your emergency.

You'd think that, at the very least, someone might offer a word of comfort or throw you a sympathetic look. But nope. Even those simple gestures seem to vanish when you're in the thick of it. It's wild, really—people you've bent over backward to help before? Suddenly, they've mastered the art of disappearing. It makes you wonder if selfishness is just baked into human nature.

So, what's the takeaway here? Live in harmony with others. Be patient, and offer help when you can. But don't expect anything in return—no compensation, no support. You've got to learn to be strong and self-reliant, standing on your own two feet.

The truth is, no one else can truly get you through tough times. It's up to you, your heart, your brain, and your hands to do the heavy lifting. And sure, you could waste time feeling bitter about other people's selfishness, but why bother? That's just the way people are. Instead, think of their ingratitude and self-interest as the water and mud of life—from which you'll rise, like a lotus flower in the morning sun, calm and unbothered by all the muck around you.

## 29. READING IS A DUTY

Never pick up a book just to kill time or entertain yourself—especially not while your mind is busy thinking about a million other things. Multitasking might work for laundry and emails, but it's a disaster when it comes to reading.

Before you dive in, do your homework. Get to know the big names, the authors who've stood the test of time, and have a clear idea of what you actually enjoy reading. Trust me, it's better to pick a well-acclaimed classic than to waste your time on something that'll make you roll your eyes halfway through. And hey, reader reviews? Those are gold. They can tell you more about a book than the blurb on the back ever will.

Once you've chosen your book, read it like you mean it—from cover to cover. None of this skimming or half-hearted flipping through pages. Reading isn't a casual thing; it's like going to see a Broadway show. You wouldn't walk out in the middle of the second act or start texting during the climax, right? Show the same respect to the author. Give the work your full attention. If you read a few pages here, a few pages there, with days in between, you're not just shortchanging yourself—you're killing the vibe of the whole experience.

And don't be afraid to read the same book more than once. In your younger years, you might speed through it for the story. But as you get older and (hopefully) wiser, read it slowly, take notes, reflect on the deeper meanings. When you're old and gray, go back to that book from your youth and marvel at how differently it speaks to you now.

Reading isn't just about passing time—it's about understanding life, filling in the gaps of what we're still unsure about, and revisiting the things that have shaped us. Plus, it's one of the few duties in life that won't make you dread Monday mornings.

# 30. LIFE'S CROSSROADS

## Loneliness Is Condolence

Happiness or sadness? It often boils down to the company you keep. If your friends, partners, bosses, or family members are mean-spirited, it's a one-way ticket to Stressville. Nothing puts a damper on life quite like family feuds or partners who turn quarrels into an Olympic sport. It's draining, depressing, and honestly, a bit of a buzzkill.

When you're surrounded by that kind of negative energy, sometimes the best solution is to retreat into your own world—just you and your thoughts. Even Tolstoy, the literary giant, decided he'd had enough and made his final exit at a railway station while running away from his wife. It turns out even great writers know when to call it quits. George Washington himself once admitted it's better to be alone than stuck in bad company. And you know what? He was onto something.

## Wavering

Then, there are those moments when life throws you a curveball and you're completely lost. You're at a crossroads, unsure of which direction to take. Nothing seems clear. Your friends, colleagues, even your closest confidants can't offer much help—probably because they're just as confused as you are. And let's be honest, sometimes their advice is more like a maze than a map.

In the end, though, you're left with one choice: rely on yourself. As the Buddha wisely said, "Be an island unto yourself" amidst the ocean of life. Sometimes, those decisions you made during your darkest hours, the ones you thought were just minor, turn out to have the biggest impact. And on the flip side, those grand plans you've spent years thinking about? They may still be sitting in the waiting room of your mind, patiently waiting their turn to come to life.

## 31. PREDESTINED FATE

Everyone's got their own path in life, from cradle to grave. When you're a kid, you're carefree, running wild without a second thought. As a grown-up, you're driven, passionate, ready to conquer the world. Then, before you know it, you hit the brakes—suddenly cautious, overthinking everything like an old cat watching a rocking chair. You've got your plans, and you start thinking you're the master of your own universe, free and creative as can be.

But here's the kicker: that's only half true.

It's like there's a master blueprint for your life, pre-drawn by some Supreme Being up there, watching from the stars. You think you're in control, but it turns out there's a whole system working behind the scenes. Every time you make a move—whether it's stumbling into a situation, crossing paths with someone who might become a friend (or enemy), or falling head over heels in love—it feels suspiciously like it was all set up ahead of time. Every triumph, every failure, every heartbreak, every hopeful new beginning—it's all been arranged for you by the Creator, God, or whoever's running the cosmic show.

There's an order to every fate.

If you're lazy and dishonest, well, don't be shocked when life hands you a pile of failures. But if you're hardworking and sincere, success is waiting for you just around the corner. If you're mean and impatient, get ready for some lonely nights. But if you're patient and willing to sacrifice, love will eventually knock on your door—probably when you least expect it.

Life's a bit like an old-school arcade game. You suffer through it with pessimism, and it'll keep throwing you obstacles, mysteries, and frustration at every turn. But show some respect for the game—treat life with a little joy and creativity, and suddenly, you're winning at it. Happiness follows those who play by the rules of positivity.

So, here's the deal: the Creator's always keeping an eye on us. He'll toss us a challenge to keep things interesting, give us a pat on the back when we get it right, and send a little cosmic punishment our way when we go off the rails.

The good news? You're still free and creative. But just remember—you're free and creative within the blueprint someone else drew up long before you even realized it.

**105**

## 32. RESPECTING OURSELVES

Some people believe life is short. Thirty-six thousand days fly by like a dream, and let's face it—most of them get eaten up by the little things: sleeping, commuting, scrolling through your phone, standing in line for coffee, going to the bathroom, talking about nothing, visiting people you don't really want to see, daydreaming about vacations you'll never take, and making grand plans you'll forget by lunchtime.

Do we even really work a full eight hours a day? Be honest. It's pretty much impossible to ask anyone to work nonstop from morning to evening without taking a breather. Time is limited, so it's worth respecting what you're doing and who you're doing it with. Life's too short to waste on people who drain your energy or hijack your time. You've got to be firm with those folks—politeness, patience, and delicate diplomacy with time-wasters? That's just slow-motion self-destruction.

Sure, some people might think you're being selfish or even a little harsh. But hey, you've got a life to live. If you want to accomplish anything worthwhile, don't let the troublemakers get too close. Skip the useless meetings, the empty chatter, and for the love of sanity, stop filling your brain with junk news.

Respecting yourself means cherishing every moment of your life. That doesn't mean you have to rush through your days or push yourself to the brink of burnout. Take things one step at a time—frequency and patience are your secret weapons for going the distance.

When you respect yourself, others will respect you too. Yes, it's great to share your time and compassion with others, but remember: you have to love and protect yourself first. After all, if you don't, who will?

## 33. NEVER SEE THE BETRAYER AGAIN

Betrayal. It's one of the most revolting, gut-wrenching evils a person can commit. Sure, murderers have to pay with their lives for what they've done, and even their crimes can be reduced, forgiven, or forgotten over time. But betrayal? That's a whole different beast.

The betrayer isn't some distant villain—they were right there beside you, sharing your life. You laughed together, broke bread together, leaned on each other during tough times, maybe even had one too many drinks together. Heck, you might've even made love to this person. That's what makes betrayal so ugly—it's the treachery from someone who knew you up close.

Here's the thing: don't waste a single moment feeling sorry for a betrayer or trying to understand them. Don't let them talk their way out of it with explanations, excuses, or a sob story about "what went wrong." It doesn't matter if they were your closest friend, your lover, or someone who meant the world to you. Once the betrayal is done, they're no longer worthy of your forgiveness or even a second glance.

If you were a nation, the betrayer would be exiled, condemned to live out their days in disgrace. But since you're just a regular human being, the best revenge is to kick them out of your life for good. Stay away, don't engage, and let them feel the weight of your absence. That's the most withering scorn you can offer— knowing they'll never have a place in your life again.

And whatever you do, never give them a hand. That kind of person doesn't deserve a spot in your world, let alone your time or help.

Time will blur the edges of many things, turning both good and bad moments into distant memories. But the sting of betrayal? That's the one curse that sticks around. It'll be there in the back of your mind, like a stubborn splinter that never quite works its way out.

## 34. OBSERVING THE PRECEPTS

I once made a solemn promise to the Buddha to follow the Five Precepts:

- *No drinking wine,*

- *No sensual misconduct,*

- *No killing,*

- *No evil tongue,*

- *No greed.*

Sounds simple, right? Not exactly. Trying to live by these rules feels like walking a tightrope over a pit of temptation. I mean, how am I supposed to stick to all of these every single day? Is there a cheat sheet somewhere?

Then I remember an old famous king and Buddhist of our country, who once spoke about *Cu tran lac dao* (roughly translated: "Finding joy in life on earth"). His advice? Pretty straightforward: eat when you're hungry, sleep when you yawn, and let life unfold as it will. Honestly, that sounds way more doable than trying to be a saint every minute of the day.

So, with a little nod to both the Buddha and that wise old king, I've come up with a slightly more... realistic version of the precepts for myself:

- Drink *less* wine. Let's aim for balance, not prohibition.

- *Appreciate beauty*, but let's dial down the lust to something more, shall we say, respectable.

- Eat *less meat* and more vegetables—gotta stay healthy, right?

- *Cut down* on speaking ill of others. Replace it with speaking gently (or at least biting my tongue).

- *Reduce greed*—hey, mindfulness is the name of the game.

- *Smile more*, frown less—anger isn't a good look on anyone.

- Keep it *simple*—life's complicated enough without my help.

So there it is—a more practical version of the precepts. The Buddha might raise an eyebrow, but I think that wise old king would approve. After all, sometimes the key to enlightenment is just knowing when to relax a little.

## 35. LONELY TRAVELER

When I was younger, I wandered from place to place like a nomad with a small briefcase stuffed with books, a little cash, and an endless curiosity. My mode of transportation? Trains. I'd bounce between European cities, shuffling through bustling platforms, sometimes making accidental companions, always chasing something I could never quite name. Sure, ahead there might be a busy avenue, cold food at some random street corner, and a shabby hotel room waiting for me—but that didn't stop me. I was hooked on the thrill of the journey.

Cities came and went. I took big steps through foreign streets, listening to the sound of my own footsteps echo in unfamiliar places. Occasionally, I'd spot roadside flowers and remember, for a brief moment, that there's beauty even in the rush. The train would glide through mountains, hills, and cities, and through the window, I'd catch glimpses of a golden forest fading into the distance, signaling that autumn had quietly replaced summer. I traveled through all four seasons, year after year, with nothing but my thoughts and a changing landscape to keep me company.

There were moments when I met people—quick friendships formed over a drink in a corner bar or in the tight quarters of a train carriage. We'd laugh, share stories, and for a while, the loneliness would ease. But then, the train would pull into the station, and we'd part ways as strangers once again.

Traveling solo has a funny way of making you feel both free and outcast at the same time. You're surrounded by fellow human beings, yet somehow, you can feel like the loneliest person on the planet. Still, despite the occasional pang of solitude, I loved it. There's a certain peace that comes with being on your own, even if the journey is sometimes cold and quiet.

I think back to when I was a kid. I used to crank the fan to full blast in the dead of winter, then burrow under the covers for a good night's sleep. It made no sense, but it felt comforting. Funny how life works—one day you'll find yourself lying alone without any shelter at all, and somehow, you'll have to make peace with that too.

## 36. THE TUG OF DREAMS AND RESISTANCE

### Dreams

Some wishes are destined to remain just that—wishes. Or maybe they're dreams, floating somewhere between reality and fantasy. Life, too, sometimes feels like a dream, slipping through our fingers without a clear explanation, like the old story of *The Nanke Dream*. We find ourselves caught up in the swirl of duties, endless problems, and the monotonous rhythm of daily life. And before we know it, we start to wonder: was that beautiful wish of ours just a dream all along?

But hey, maybe that's the point. Maybe dreams are meant to exist on the edge of our reality, keeping life just interesting enough to make us chase them, even when we know they're a little out of reach.

### Wishes and Resistance

The sky's the limit when it comes to human intentions—sometimes our wishes are wild and dreamy, sometimes they're pressing and urgent. They can be as unpredictable as a summer storm. Our intentions shift with time, and what we want one day might look completely different the next.

But here's the twist: every time we have a new wish or plan, there's that nagging inner voice—resistance. When we're young, that voice is just a whisper, easily drowned out by our enthusiasm and determination. We charge forward, fueled by our desires. But as we get older, that voice grows louder, and suddenly, we're more cautious. We start weighing our choices, second-guessing our dreams, and slowing down before we make our next move.

The funny thing is, that voice of resistance doesn't care whether your wish is good or bad, noble or selfish. It's always there, making you pause and think. And the line between good and bad, mercy and malice? It's thinner than you might think. What feels right to you might be seen differently by someone else—or by society at large.

In the end, the balance between your dreams and resistance determines the path you walk. Early on, you listen to your dreams, moving quickly, chasing after what you want without much hesitation. But as time goes on, you start listening to that inner resistance, walking more slowly, taking time to think before making decisions. Life's four seasons come and go at the same pace, but somehow, time seems to speed up as you get older.

So maybe the secret is this: live without too many wishes or ambitions. Don't waste your energy fighting others or even yourself. Do you feel happier when you let go of the struggle and embrace being carefree? Maybe that's the real dream.

# 37. THE REAL PURSUIT

## *Happy Things in a Day*

It's the small, seemingly insignificant moments that often bring the most joy. Like going home for lunch with your parents, bringing along a little gift, serving them with your chopsticks, and chatting about the good old days. Or after a sweltering, exhausting day when the power's out and you're drenched in sweat, a heavy rainstorm finally rolls in. You feel the cool wind through the windows, and the streets begin to flood. You pack up your things, call your spouse to say you're coming home, and by the time you walk through the door, the family is gathered in the kitchen. You open a bottle of wine, laugh with the kids, and let the day's troubles stay outside with the rain.

Happiness often sneaks up on us in these simple moments. Despite the chaos of life, it's these everyday experiences that remind us to be present and find joy in what we have right in front of us.

## *Success and Happiness*

We're all chasing success, but here's the tricky part: success is measured by society's ever-changing standards—standards we can't always control. We make wise choices, take action, and do our best, but success is like a moving target. What society celebrates today might change tomorrow.

Happiness, though, is a different story. It doesn't depend on society's approval—it comes from within. True happiness isn't about reaching some external goal; it's about finding peace in your own heart. And that's something only you can control.

If you want lasting happiness, stop focusing on changing everything outside of yourself. Instead, turn inward. Change your perspective, adjust your expectations, and cultivate peace in your own soul. It takes practice, but when your inner world is at peace, happiness becomes a constant companion.

While success is fleeting, happiness—true, deep happiness—is something that grows from within and lasts a lifetime.

### The Real Pursuit

Success may come and go, but happiness is found in those small moments—like a quiet family dinner after a long day, or the feeling of peace that comes from letting go of the world's chaos. True happiness isn't something you chase; it's something you create from within. And that's a pursuit worth every moment.

## 38. HUMAN LIFE

One day, it hits you—life is hard and tiring. You're lugging around this massive load filled with responsibilities, unfulfilled wishes, grudges you can't shake, obligations that feel fake, pointless opposition, embarrassing failures, and a bunch of other trivial nonsense that somehow weighs a ton.

You dream of putting it all down—just dropping that burden and walking away, free and easy. Or maybe, if you're lucky, you can just stop altogether and catch your breath.

But then, reality sets in. I've realized why I can't stop or shrug off the load. All the stress, problems, exhaustion, and loneliness—well, that's life, isn't it? It's part of the package. Carrying it around feels like my responsibility, maybe even my duty, to repay the universe for letting me have this life in the first place. There's no escape from that.

More than once, I've hit that wall of depression, where no matter what I did, I couldn't change anything. I felt like a bee, buzzing frantically, repeatedly slamming into a closed window trying to get out—only to fail over and over again.

But here's what I've learned from those moments: sometimes, the only way forward is to stay calm and wait. The chaos eventually settles. An opportunity appears, and if you're patient, a new door opens, leading you down a different path.

So, keep going. Keep carrying that heavy load, even when it feels unbearable. The right moments will come when they're meant to, and only when you've lived your full life can you finally set everything down for good.

I said as much to the dead bee on the windowsill—it had been too hasty and panicked to notice I had already opened the window for it.

## 39. THE PUSH AND PULL OF LIFE

### *Whispering to Yourself*

It seems like everyone I meet these days—friends, acquaintances, state employees, businesspeople, students—they're all caught in this web of insecurity. They're waiting for something, or someone, to make a move and fix things. But here's the hard truth: nothing's going to magically change. The world keeps spinning, and most things stay exactly as they are.

Take a look at some organizations. Instead of thriving on talent, they prop up loudmouths and faction cheerleaders. Spoiler alert: they won't last long. It's like watching a slow-motion train wreck, and yes, you only need to glance at a few of our neighboring countries to see how this plays out. It's depressing—time flies, and while you're stuck in a system that's broken, your creativity and energy get slowly ground down into dust. All those grand plans and ambitions? They start to feel like pipe dreams.

There have been so many times I've wanted to just give up. I've fantasized about retreating, writing a book, or maybe becoming a teacher. But then that restless fire from my younger days flares up again. So, if the timing's right, I'll fight like a man should. But if luck decides to pass me by, I'm perfectly fine staying at home, letting go of the big dreams, and diving into the scriptures for some much-needed peace and perspective.

### *Being Kind*

Here's the thing: the Earth isn't as big as it feels. You never know when you'll cross paths with old acquaintances—or worse, people who know your old acquaintances. So, why not live a moral life? Do your best to avoid harming others, and don't waste your breath speaking ill of them. Whenever you can, be kind. You might not run into those same people again, but you might meet someone who knows them. And here's the kicker: being kind to someone is like planting a seed. Eventually, you get to enjoy the reputation that kindness brings—it's an investment that never loses value.

Life pulls you in all directions—between wanting to give up and feeling that youthful fire to keep going. But no matter which path you take, one rule stays true: be kind. Even when the world doesn't change, even when your ambitions feel out of reach, your kindness will come back to you in ways you can't predict. And in the end, that's the legacy worth leaving behind.

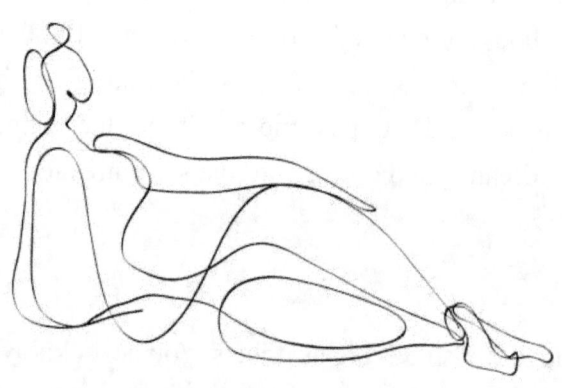

## 40. THE MEANING OF LIFE

Maybe the big question—"What's the meaning of life?"—only really gets answered at the very end. It's like the punchline to a joke that takes decades to set up. But trying to figure it out now? Well, that's tricky business.

So, what's life about anyway? Is it about making piles of money so you can buy everything your heart desires? The fancy car, the latest gadgets, traveling to all the Instagram-worthy places?

Honestly, you don't need all that much. Enough is good. Nearly enough? That's even better. For me, money is best spent on good books. If I have a little extra, maybe I'll grab some great music. If I'm feeling really flush, I'll spring for some nice wine to share with friends. That's about the extent of my wild dreams.

Or maybe it's all about fame—being that person who's respected and admired, with people waiting on you hand and foot.

But let's be real—that's just vanity talking!

As I see it, the meaning of life boils down to something simpler: helping those in need and doing what we can to make the people around us happy. It's about being honest with yourself—no lies, no harm, no nonsense.

Sure, it sounds simple. But trust me, it's a lot harder to pull off than it seems. The meaning of your life isn't something that magically appears when you're gone. You work it out right here, while you're living it.

## 41. PROPERTY IS A BURDEN

As the years pass, we accumulate all sorts of stuff—at home, at the office, in closets, and on shelves. Most of it just sits there, collecting dust. If you were to wander around your house right now and peek into the forgotten corners, you'd probably find all kinds of random things you haven't touched in years.

Whenever we pack for a trip, we cram our suitcases with "just-in-case" items, things we never end up using but that do a great job of making our shoulders ache.

We chase after things for validation—thinking more stuff equals more happiness. But the truth is, those possessions rarely bring lasting joy. Instead, they pile up around us, more like clutter than treasure, serving as little more than decoration or temporary emotional spikes.

Just like we need regular showers to stay fresh, our rooms need regular cleaning to stay sane. A good decluttering session can be a breath of fresh air, literally. Imagine a clean kitchen with an almost empty fridge that holds just the essentials—no more expired yogurt containers hiding in the back. Old magazines? Toss 'em. Random papers you swear you'll get to someday? Time to let go.

And it's not just physical clutter that weighs us down. You've got to clear out the mental junk, too—those pointless worries, overblown goals, and interests that lead you in circles. Trim the excess and focus on the now, with practical simplicity.

A simple meal—steamed rice, sesame salt, some vegetables, maybe a bowl of thick soy sauce—tastes surprisingly good when you slow down to really enjoy it. And nothing feels better than setting off on a new adventure with only the essentials in your bag. It's light, it's liberating, and your shoulders will thank you.

# 42. LIVING FULLY, ONE SMALL STEP AT A TIME

## *How to Live*

Steve Jobs once embraced a Zen idea: live each day as if it were your last. Sounds dramatic, right? But the wisdom behind it is simple. When you know your time is limited, everything around you takes on new meaning.

For your family, you care more deeply, for your enemies, you find it easier to let go. You start noticing the little things in nature that you used to walk right past. And what about yourself? You quickly realize that with limited time, you can't do *everything*. Instead, you focus on the *one* thing that matters most to you and give it your all.

Living like this strips away the distractions. There's no room for wasting time on things that don't light you up. If you can carry that mindset throughout your entire life, you'll find yourself living more fully—slow, focused, and satisfied. Suddenly, even the smallest moments become precious.

## *Reality*

Let's get practical. There's something powerful in simply *getting things done*, even if they're small. Completing a minor task beats leaving a grand plan gathering dust.

And when it comes to success, stumbling your way through mistakes is far better than holding onto a flawless plan that never sees the light of day. Reality isn't about perfect blueprints—it's about rolling up your sleeves and making progress, one imperfect step at a time.

## *The Art of Living*

The key to a full life is simpler than we think. Focus on what matters most, cherish the small moments, and keep moving forward, even if your steps aren't perfect. Life isn't about grand, unfinished plans—it's about living each day fully and turning even small victories into meaningful progress.

## 43. POINTS OF VIEW AND PERSONALITY

When you're a leader, the way you evaluate your staff isn't exactly the same way they evaluate each other. Your perspective shifts. And let's be real—how a man sees a woman often has very little to do with how she sees herself. As a parent? Well, you'll almost always be harder on your kids than they are on themselves, even if they think they're being tough.

Here's the kicker: evaluating people isn't easy. The minute you think you've got someone all figured out, you're probably not being as objective as you think. People are like chameleons—how they act depends on the situation, the time of day, maybe even how much sleep they got last night. And, truth be told, your viewpoint changes just as much as theirs.

That's why human society can feel like a giant, ever-shifting kaleidoscope. The best approach? Learn to observe, listen, and accept people as they are, without rushing to judgment. If sharing your thoughts is necessary, do it without a verdict attached. After all, we're all just trying to figure it out as we go.

Take last night, for example. My daughter was sobbing because I'd scolded her for not focusing on her work. In the midst of her tears, she hit me with this: "It's all your fault! You don't care about the family enough!" That stopped me in my tracks. I took a deep breath and listened. And you know what? She wasn't entirely wrong. Kids have this brutal honesty that makes you reflect on your own behavior. It reminded me that sometimes, the best human traits are the simplest: straightforwardness and sincerity.

## 44. HARD-TO-EXPLAIN STUFF

As time goes by, you'll get a little wiser—age and experience have a funny way of doing that. You start treating the world with a bit more grace, stop asking those cringe-worthy questions, and hopefully cut back on doing silly things.

But here's the kicker: you'll probably never stop questioning *yourself*. If anything, you become the biggest mystery you'll ever try to solve. You'll spend a lifetime wondering about your own desires, intentions, and why on earth you make the choices you do.

The thing is, each of us has a path—a fate or destiny that's been set from the moment we're born. Everything we do revolves around this axis, even when it feels like we're spinning off into chaos.

Figuring out your path means figuring out *you*. It's the moment when the puzzle pieces click into place, and you realize what you're doing, why you're doing it, and where it's all leading. That little spark of awareness? That's enlightenment.

Of course, staying on track isn't a one-and-done deal. You've got to practice mindfulness, keep yourself grounded, and do your best to stay aligned with that path. But hey, no one said understanding yourself was going to be easy—it's a lifelong adventure with plenty of "hard-to-explain stuff" along the way.

## 45. BODY AND MIND

### *The Structure of Human Beings*

We humans are made up of four parts: body, mind, emotion, and spirit. But let's be honest—we often treat our minds like the star of the show, spending endless hours on mental development, while riding the emotional rollercoaster that life throws at us. And when we're in a good mood? Well, that's when we start talking about spirit and belief with a reverence usually reserved for Sunday mornings.

But then there's our body. This bag of flesh and bones that keeps us alive is often an afterthought. We expect it to just keep going, day after day, like a loyal servant who never complains. That is, until it starts complaining. Maybe it's a stiff back from bad posture or a cold that knocks us out of commission, but it's only when the body decides to go on strike that we suddenly start paying attention. And when illness hits hard enough to sweep away everything else, we're forced to realize just how much we've been neglecting it. By then? It's often too late.

The key, as I see it, is balance. Give all four parts—body, mind, emotion, and spirit—equal attention. Don't treat any one part like it's just along for the ride. Keep them all in harmony, and maybe your body won't have to resort to giving you a wake-up call with aches and pains.

### *Why We Go to the Massage*

Let's face it: sometimes life just beats us down. We get lonely, anxious, or stressed, and suddenly we're like little animals groaning in misery. In those moments, a gentle hand—whether it's a friend's comforting words or a good old-fashioned back rub—can work wonders.

That's where the spa or a massage comes in. It's like hitting the reset button or popping a pain-relieving tablet, but much more enjoyable. Sure, it's not going to fix all your problems, but it's a quick remedy for feeling like the world is too much to handle.

Unless you're one of those rare people who's always successful, always content, and never stressed out—if that's you, congratulations, you don't need this advice. But for the rest of us? A little pampering goes a long way.

## *The Balance*

When life gets overwhelming, balance is everything. We need to take care of our body just as much as we do our mind, emotions, and spirit. And when that balance tips and we find ourselves sinking into stress or exhaustion, sometimes all it takes is a little self-care—whether it's a massage, a spa day, or simply acknowledging that we can't do it all. After all, nobody's perfect—and that's exactly why we all need a reset every now and then.

# 46. FAITH AND THE ETERNAL UNIVERSE

## *Faith*

There are so many things in this world that we just can't wrap our heads around—whether it's in the sky, on the ground, or within our own hearts. Our souls are intertwined with the universe in ways we can't always explain. So, you shouldn't be too shocked when your prayers come true or when someone's astrological chart lines up with their life story like a cosmic GPS. It's all a bit of a miracle, really.

And that's why we need to believe in and respect the sacred, even when it's beyond our understanding. This is the essence of faith—believing in something bigger than ourselves, even when we can't fully comprehend it. But there's a line. Don't go off the deep end with superstition or become obsessed with fortune-tellers or shamans. That's a sure way to spiral into confusion and lose your grip on reality.

Sure, there are different worlds—ghosts, devils, fairies, Buddhas, and saints. They exist alongside us, brushing against our lives here and there. But here's the deal: while we're still walking this earth as humans, we've got to focus on living this life—feet on the ground, eyes on the road ahead, and tackling the daily grind as best we can.

## *Gods and Deities*

Our bodies? They start out as tiny little things, growing from a fetus into the people we become—walking, talking, learning, and eventually, growing old and returning to dust. The physical part of us has an expiration date, no matter how much we might want to do something immortal or chase after the fountain of youth.

But here's the twist: while our bodies fade, our souls stick around. Our souls are tied to the world itself—the mountains, rivers, fields, and lakes. We're part of something much bigger than just our physical form. And when our time comes, it's our soul that joins the eternal universe, merging with the realm of deities.

This understanding only really sinks in when we let go of our ego—our assumptions about ourselves, our arrogance, and the mistakes we make trying to convince ourselves that we're bigger than we are. Humility in this world and reverence for the divine—that's where truth lies.

### The Balance of Faith and Humility

In a world filled with mysteries we'll never fully understand, faith is about accepting what's sacred and beyond our reach, without letting superstition take over. While our bodies may come and go, our souls remain part of the eternal universe. So, walk humbly on this earth, respect the deities, and focus on living with a sense of balance between the here and now and the infinite beyond.

## 47. TAKE YOUR STEP

What are you really looking for in this life? What does your soul crave?

Every day, when you wake up and realize you're still healthy, you start thinking about your next move. Whether it's work, a new plan, or some unfinished business, you set out on your path—sometimes slowly, sometimes in a hurry. Maybe you stick to the familiar route, or maybe you venture into new territory. But here's the question: why are you walking that path in the first place?

If your goal is money, fame, or power, well, buckle up—it's going to be a long and bumpy road. You'll have your fair share of scheming, winning, losing, and plenty of suffering along the way. And let's be honest, that's the price of admission for chasing those things.

Sure, along the way you'll catch some fleeting pleasures. A reunion with old friends, a chance encounter with a beautiful stranger, a glass of fine wine, or maybe a cigarette paired with an irresistible song. For a moment, it all feels like the universe is handing you a treat, tailor-made for your enjoyment.

But here's the catch—those moments of pleasure? They're just brief flashes. They don't stick around. They leave you with nothing but a hollow space, a tired body, and an even more restless soul.

So your lust for life is temporarily satisfied. But is that really all you need? Why is it that after all the excitement, you still feel empty? Are you wasting your time chasing things that don't last? Deep down, are you still...sad? It seems like you're searching for something more, doesn't it?

As a traveler in life, the truth is simple: you've got to take your step. But don't just follow any path blindly. Listen to your soul. It's trying to tell you what it really wants. And once you figure that out, that's the path you should be following.

## 48. IF TOMORROW NEVER CAME

In your twenties or thirties, death feels like a distant concept, something reserved for old age. Life keeps rolling, and you just keep moving forward, feeling invincible. You might even think, "*Eh, I just need to make it to 60.*" After all, people in their sixties? They're practically half-asleep, right?

But then you hit your forties, and suddenly, a few old acquaintances start passing away. You feel a shiver down your spine. When winter rolls around, your body seems to fall apart at the first cold snap—whether it's a mild cold or something that knocks you flat. Your body's not the well-oiled machine it used to be. By the time you approach 50, ambition starts to fade a little. Two or three decades have flown by in the blink of an eye, and you've still got a pile of unfinished plans. It dawns on you: there's no way you'll get all that time back.

Deep down, you realize that you've probably only got a solid 10 years left to really work. Death could show up at any time. No one can predict it. I've seen plenty of healthy-looking folks, the kind who seem full of life, take a sudden nosedive after a routine doctor's visit. One checkup later, they've been handed the news: their time is almost up.

But let's be honest—daily life keeps us so busy with its endless worries and hassles that we rarely stop to think about death. Who has time to contemplate their mortality when there's laundry to fold and bills to pay?

That's why I think we should all ask ourselves a question at least once a year: *If I had only seven days left to live, what would I do? What would I let go of? Who would I care about, and what would I do for them?*

You know you're not a saint—just an ordinary person who's made plenty of mistakes. But with seven days left, you'd have to let go of the past, maybe even release some of that grudge you've held onto for years. Sure, there'd be debts to settle, but who could manage all that in a week? So, you'd focus on what really matters. A few important people. A few important tasks. The things that are truly invaluable. Everything else? It would reveal itself to be trivial, easily forgotten.

In the end, you'd realize—*Hey, I've been chasing all the wrong things.* And just like that, you'd be enlightened.

127

## 49. LUST

We often talk about lust like it's something dirty—something we should banish from our lives entirely. But let me ask you this: is there such a thing as *noble* lust? When does lust suddenly become virtuous?

It's all just a word game, really. Lust isn't limited to the stuff we try to avoid talking about at family dinners. Lust is simply everything we want in life. And let's be honest, as long as you're alive, you've got some kind of lust pulling you along. Giving it up entirely? Not going to happen. Lust shapes who you are. It's woven into your actions, your desires, your drive to live.

The Buddha nailed it when he said that ignorance, greed, and anger are the root causes of all suffering. So yes, overcoming lust is part of finding true peace. But let's not kid ourselves—lust is also what pushes us to act. Whether you're hustling at work or just daydreaming on the couch, it's all driven by some form of lust.

The only time you're truly free from lust? When you're six feet under. Until then, you might as well accept that lust is part of life.

But here's the trick—don't fight it, just keep it in check. The key is balance. Figure out who you are and what type of passion suits you. The secret isn't in eliminating lust; it's knowing when to dial it down and when to let it fuel you.

There's no such thing as noble or despicable passion—it's all about what fits with your character and your current situation. So instead of waging war on your lust, embrace it. Just make sure it's working *for* you, not against you.

## 50. INDIFFERENCE AND CURIOSITY

In modern society, we've got way too much on our plates—so many things to think about, worry about, and stress over. National education teaches us to focus on results, not on emotions. We see injustice and silly mistakes happening left and right, but nothing seems to change. Life feels like it's spinning in the same old tired cycle. It's no wonder people are becoming more and more indifferent.

Take doctors, for example. They've got to follow the treatment process by the book, so they become indifferent to their patients' pain. Traffic cops? They're more focused on handing out tickets than dealing with the actual casualties. And let's be honest, how many of us skip over the charity columns in the news and go straight to the juicy stories about money and scandal? Indifference has found its way into the very corners of political and religious life—where love and compassion should be front and center. Meanwhile, the government's complex, bloated system churns out leaders who turn a blind eye to the suffering of everyday people. And don't even get me started on those giant new pagodas popping up like tourist traps.

On the flip side, we're more curious than ever. With today's endless media outlets, we've got access to all the information we could ever want. We can look into every corner of life, dig up facts, and share what we learn with the click of a button. We're hungry for knowledge, searching with a kind of fervor. But here's the irony: the more we know, the more indifferent we seem to become.

## 51. GLOOMY DAY

Some days, life just feels like one long sigh. You wake up already exhausted, wanting nothing more than to pull the covers over your head and call it a day before it even starts. You don't want to deal with people, responsibilities, or anything that requires moving from your cozy spot. If it were possible, you'd pack up and disappear to some far-off place where no one knows your name—a magical land where stress, sadness, and annoying phone calls don't exist.

On days like this, it feels like the universe is conspiring against you. Every little thing seems poised to crash down—whether it's a phone call you've been dreading, a knock at the door you're not ready for, or some vague sense of impending doom. It's like everything's watching you, just waiting for the right moment to pounce.

In these moments, you can't help but reflect on life—and not in a good way. You look at your days and wonder what the point of it all is. Everything feels empty, like it's lost its meaning. You want to scream, throw something, or maybe just have a good cry. But instead, you lie there, still as a rock, hoping that if you don't move, the world might just forget you're there.

## 52. RESTIVE PASSION

Passion is the fuel behind every move we make—whether we're doing something noble or something we probably shouldn't. That passion for sensual delight? Yeah, it sticks with you for life. Then there's the passion for beauty, which pushes us to create, to strive for something more, to seek perfection.

A life without passion? That's like walking down a pitch-black road with no end in sight. It's dull, it's empty, and it's definitely not a place you want to be.

But here's the tricky part: too much passion can blow up in your face. It's like trying to tame a wildfire with a garden hose—good luck. Passion is instinctual, and it's always there, smoldering beneath the surface, just waiting for the right moment to catch fire.

Even monks, who've sworn off worldly pleasures, aren't immune to it. They still have dreams, wet or otherwise, because, let's be real, no one's completely free from desire. The trick isn't to eliminate passion—it's to find balance. Dedicate yourself to something meaningful, and don't let your passions run wild. Keep that fire controlled. Sure, passion is a good motivator, but too much of it can burn you out. Stay on course, keep your cool, and let passion work for you, not against you.

## 53. HANGING OUT WITH FRIENDS

Let's face it—people can't survive in isolation forever. Even the most introverted among us need some form of human connection. If we had no one to share with, to talk to, we'd practically disappear. We're wired to communicate. It's why we crave get-togethers—to share a laugh, to be heard, or sometimes just to hear the reassuring hum of conversation around us.

We hang out for all sorts of reasons: to show off a bit, gather a support crew, escape loneliness, or maybe just satisfy some passing curiosity. But here's the golden rule: never hang out just because you're trying to mimic someone else's life. You'll end up bored, and worse—boring.

The secret to good company? Use your ears more than your mouth. You'd be surprised how much you can learn when you stop talking and start listening. Humility and a good sense of humor will take you much further than being loud and boastful.

Some people hang out just for the sake of it—even when they don't really want to. And plenty of folks, whether they're know-it-alls or know-nothings, love to show off. The problem is, they usually aren't learning anything—they're too busy being impressed with themselves. But here's the upside: if you pay attention, even the biggest braggarts can teach you something (even if it's what *not* to do).

That said, we don't have endless time to waste. Be smart with yours. Don't fill your calendar with constant social outings. Catch up with old friends once or twice a year—that's plenty. And trust me, a meaningful conversation with someone wiser is far more valuable than spending hours at some superficial, show-off gathering.

## 54. THE BRAGGER

Braggers are everywhere—like moths to a flame, they're drawn to any crowd that's ready to listen. And let's be honest, the crowd is just as eager to have them. People, by nature, are often gullible and crave belonging. They don't want to stand out awkwardly in a crowd—they want to blend in, to be part of something, even if it's just for a moment at a party or meeting. So, they wait for someone to take charge of the conversation, someone to dazzle them. Enter the bragger.

This bragger doesn't need much—a captive audience and a half-decent memory for stories, real or invented. He's witty, or at least thinks he is, and his so-called "achievements" from the past are trotted out like prized show ponies. The crowd, feeling fortunate to have someone "special" among them, eats it up. For that brief window of time, everyone feels proud to be in the presence of such greatness.

The bragger? He's in his element. He talks more than anyone else, holding court like he's the star of the show. But here's the thing—he's also watching. If someone dares to look disinterested or doesn't hang on his every word, he'll notice. His mood will shift. He'll either pull back or double down, depending on whether or not he's getting the attention he craves. He's got stories for days—some funny, some not, and some you've heard three times already at different gatherings. But he doesn't care. He's there to be the center of attention, the "soul" of the event, and he'll talk big until he's satisfied.

Your best bet? Stay clear of the bragger and the endless string of pointless gatherings where he thrives. Life's too short to get stuck in the same tired conversations with someone who's more interested in hearing himself talk than engaging with anyone else.

## 55. TWO SIDES OF THE SAME COIN

### Two Sides

Life, as you might've noticed, has a funny way of showing its duality. Look closely enough, and you'll see that every seemingly straightforward action often has a flip side. A person can appear warm and welcoming, but beneath that surface, there might be a layer of indifference. Kindness can be masked by formality, and bold, risky behavior might actually be driven by deep-seated cowardice. Even that generous donation? Sometimes it's just a cover for stinginess.

It's a bit like a plant growing next to a poisonous mushroom—learning to tolerate the toxicity. People, too, carry opposing characteristics, and depending on the situation, either side can show itself.

The trick, of course, is to understand this as part of human nature. The truly intelligent person isn't fooled by surface-level actions. They see through the charade and understand what's driving those behaviors. Life's full of contradictions, and knowing that helps you better control the situation—and yourself.

### A Strange Thing

Happiness and sorrow—they're like two sides of the same coin, forever linked. You can't fully appreciate happiness if you haven't spent some time sitting with sorrow. Sorrow shows up when our efforts fail or when reason lets us down. But happiness? It's that lightness, that emotion we chase after—yet it wouldn't exist without its counterpart.

Here's the twist: humans tend to act on either their emotions or their reason. You can reason your way to success, but that's only part of the equation for finding happiness. Real delight comes when you've flown high enough to know what it feels like to soar above it all.

Ultimately, balance is key. When you can harmonize both your mind and your heart, that's when you've truly got control—not just of your emotions, but of life itself.

## *The Balance*

Life is a constant balancing act between opposites: warmth and indifference, kindness and formality, happiness and sorrow. To truly understand and experience life's highs, you have to acknowledge its lows. And once you strike that balance between your heart and your mind, you're in control—not just of your actions, but of how you experience everything life throws your way.

## 56. EXPERIENCE AND TRANQUILITY

Experienced people are like walking encyclopedias—they've built up a storehouse of knowledge and developed a solid dose of common sense along the way. Sure, everyone's on their own life journey, but let's be honest, some dive headfirst into the deep end, while others barely get their feet wet. It's the ones who really throw themselves into life who gather the richest experiences. They don't get rattled by every bump in the road; instead, they handle life's curveballs with a cool head and a calm heart.

When the unexpected happens—whether it's a minor hiccup or a full-blown crisis—they don't flinch. No desperate screams, no panic attacks. They watch, they analyze, and they stay quiet. Over time, they become the kind of people who see the bigger picture and find clarity where others only find chaos.

It's like a glass of water that's been shaken up—at first, everything's swirling around, but give it a moment, and all the sediment settles at the bottom. The water clears, and peace takes over. That's what happens to your mind when you sit in meditation. Slowly but surely, your thoughts settle, and wisdom rises to the surface. You learn to stay calm, no matter what life throws at you.

True peace comes when you let go of the constant chase—no more excessive lust for what you don't have, no more competing just for the sake of winning. When you start accepting life as it is, that's when you begin to feel a sense of calm and bliss creeping into your days. And from there, life flows a little smoother.

## 57. USEFUL ILLNESS

When we're young, we don't give illness a second thought. We dive into life headfirst, full of energy and passion, thinking we can conquer it all. We stumble, sure, but we bounce back quickly. In those days, we waste a lot—effort, brainpower, emotions, money, time, and yep, even our health.

Then, out of nowhere, illness drops by like an uninvited guest. It doesn't call ahead—it just shows up, like Death's way of sending a little "hello." How often this guest returns depends largely on how you treat yourself.

If you're burning the candle at both ends—working too hard, loving carelessly, scheming nonstop, drinking like you're still 21, or indulging every whim—you're asking for trouble. Sooner or later, something inside of you, or in your life, is going to snap.

That's where illness comes in handy. It forces you to hit pause, take stock of things, and (hopefully) learn a few lessons along the way. It humbles you, makes you a little wiser, and reminds you to adjust—to find your balance with Nature and yourself.

No one wants to meet Death too early, especially when you've still got unfinished business, a pile of regrets, and nothing to show for it but some crumpled bills and fleeting glory. So yes, illness can be useful. It's life's way of slapping the brakes on you before you crash.

Just don't ride those brakes too hard, though. A little illness now and then is fine— but you don't want to overdo it!

## 58. LONELINESS AS A DELIGHT

Practicing the Buddha's teachings in the middle of everyday chaos? Let's just say it's not exactly a walk in the park. Achieving a peaceful mind or awakening your soul while juggling work, social obligations, and the endless noise of life feels like trying to meditate in the middle of a rock concert. That's why monks often retreat to the mountains or deep into the forest, where the only thing bothering them might be a curious squirrel.

But here's the thing: the ultimate goal of any religion is to help people find true happiness and lead lives of selfless service. Even monks and priests can't stay in isolation forever—they eventually come back to share their wisdom with the rest of us. Just look at Buddha. The Awakened One didn't just sit under a tree forever; he hit the road as a mendicant, delivering sermons, and gathering disciples to spread the Dharma.

Still, a little solitude goes a long way. Taking time to withdraw from the hustle and bustle and dive deep into your own thoughts is not just necessary—it's delightful. Yes, you might become the subject of gossip for being "weird" or "selfish" because you enjoy your alone time. But don't worry about it; that's just the price of peace.

Like a monk, you can split your life into moments of quiet reflection, moments of work, and moments of service. The beauty is, you don't have to head to the forest or scale a mountain to do it. You can be your own oasis—right where you are. But to tap into that inner well of joy, you need to embrace solitude. Accept it, even celebrate it. Become a hermit in your own life, and discover the deep joy that comes from within.

## 59. INDIFFERENT BEAUTY

There's no denying it—women's beauty has a way of shaking the world and sparking desire. We tend to pair beauty with youth, not old age, like they're inseparable partners in crime. Youth and beauty are like sweet honey—everyone craves a taste.

It's rare, it's fleeting, and it's the reason people go to great lengths to outdo one another. Those sweet moments of beauty don't last long, so we often hope to hold onto them, sometimes even wanting to lock them away for safekeeping. But beauty doesn't work that way. Like a flower in nature, it fades—no matter how tightly you try to hold on.

When we're in love, we cherish that beauty, taking care of it like a precious treasure. And when we're hurt, we seek comfort in it, hoping it'll heal us, warm us. But here's the kicker: the Creator has a strict policy on beauty. It's fleeting, and chasing it is like trying to catch sunlight in your hands. Sure, it's dazzling, but try leaning on a beam of sunlight for support—it won't happen. Beauty is as elusive and cool as it is enchanting.

Yet, beauty is essential to life. Like sunlight and flowers, it brings warmth and brightness to our days. The trick is to welcome it with open arms, appreciating its delicacy without trying to possess it. Let it purify your soul, but don't expect it to do more than that.

In the end, beauty teaches us to live modestly. It's a gift to be enjoyed, not owned. So, enjoy it for what it is, and don't ask for more than it can give.

## 60. THE CONFIDENCE OF ARROGANCE

Why do we feel the need to show off our wisdom, knowledge, or that one special talent? Be honest—you're craving a round of applause, a bit of praise, maybe even some admiration. Who doesn't want to be the star of the show now and then? Vanity is sweet, no doubt about it—it's like candy for the ego.

But here's the catch: after the compliments fade, it's like the spotlight suddenly goes dark, and you're left standing there, blinking into the void. That's when it hits you. The applause dies down, and what's left behind are feelings of emptiness and solitude, lurking in the shadows of your arrogance. Those brief moments of showing off leave you feeling a little ridiculous, a little lost, and maybe even a little sad.

You retreat into stillness, take a good hard look at yourself, and realize you've been basking in guilty delights. There's regret, and you swear—*never again.* You'll avoid the arrogance trap, right? But let's be real—life has a funny way of bringing these things back around. Arrogance is a stubborn beast, and most of our failures can be traced right back to it. Even when we know better, we still trip over our own inflated egos.

Learning modesty takes guts, effort, and more than a few stumbles along the way. And guess what? You don't get there without failing a few times and gathering some hard-earned experience.

You're not a saint, and no one expects you to be pure of mind in a world that practically runs on vanity. Every now and then, you might need to step back, embrace a little solitude, and find some peace away from it all. So if someone calls you arrogant, don't take it too hard. It's all part of the human experience—just another lesson on the road to humility.

## 61. AGREEMENT WITH NATURE

Autumn blows in with its cool northwesterly winds, shaking a few leaves loose and nudging us to pause for a moment in the middle of our daily grind. Spring, on the other hand, whispers, "Get outside, have some fun!" Winter makes us a bit more cautious, and summer? Well, summer gets us all fired up, ready to tackle the world.

Life's not so different. Sometimes it's full of energy and excitement; other times, it feels quiet, lonely, or downright confusing. There are moments of exploration and moments of sluggish indifference. But the thing is, our feelings and nature? They're in sync, moving to the same rhythm.

If we pay attention, we'll realize that everyone and everything around us is sending signals—whether it's the weather shifting, that random dizzy spell, or a creaky knee. They're all trying to tell us something's up.

It's the voice of Nature speaking, and if you're smart, you'll listen.

You have to tune in—not just to the people around you, but to nature itself, and most importantly, to that little voice inside of you. Nature isn't something to be fought with; it's a partnership, a voluntary agreement. And it's pretty clear—if you try to go against it, nature will humble you real quick.

When you lose your temper, feel overwhelmed, or get that pounding headache that won't quit, it's usually a sign that you've broken your agreement with nature. You've strayed from the path it's laid out for you.

That's why even the smartest people can sometimes crash and burn, all because they tried to outsmart nature. Meanwhile, folks with a more modest approach seem to glide through life. Why? They've learned the secret—live in harmony with nature. It's the only way to thrive.

## 62. FORBIDDEN THINGS ARE ALWAYS TEMPTING

Life is like a fast-moving river, sweeping us along with all its twists and turns. We hardly get a chance to stop and think, and before we know it, we're realizing that we've dropped the ball—whether it's not caring enough for our family, neglecting our health until we get sick, doing something incredibly dumb, or letting our passions fall by the wayside while we're busy trying to make a living.

So, every now and then, I get the bright idea to sit down and lay out some principles for my life. I craft a detailed plan, complete with daily and weekly schedules. I promise to eat less meat, more vegetables. I set up a morning exercise routine, list things I *must* do for my family, and—of course—I make a list of all the forbidden things I'm determined to avoid.

Knowing myself, and how easily I give in to temptation, I stick these principles everywhere—on the fridge, by my desk, in the bathroom, even on my nightstand. I practically wallpaper my life with reminders.

But here's the truth: I hardly ever follow them. Life is unpredictable, full of unexpected twists, and let's be real—doing what you *should* do can be downright boring.

Getting up early for morning exercises? Ugh. Spending endless hours with family? Well, that can test anyone's patience. Reading a book? That just makes me sleepy. And let's not even talk about eating vegetables day in and day out—I'm over it after three salads.

Then, of course, when I meet up with old friends, I find myself breaking all my rules—getting drunk, smoking again, and basically tossing my principles out the window. And when I'm invited to a feast with perfectly cooked beef, velvet-smooth wine, and decadent foie gras? Forget it. I'm caving in.

We know these things aren't good for us, but we do them anyway. And then, one day, a beautiful woman crosses your path. She's got that perfect smile, eyes that seem to sparkle with mischief, and a way of moving that's just... captivating. She's modest, yet somehow incredibly tempting, shy but inviting.

Let's face it—what we shouldn't do is always the most tempting.

142

## 63. THE LAWS OF LIFE

Life has a way of keeping us on our toes—just like the weather. One day it's blazing hot, the next day it's pouring rain. Spring comes along with its hopeful buds and blossoms, while autumn turns everything golden and nostalgic. Some nights seem to drag on forever, colorless and tasteless, and then there are those magical nights, with the moonlight shining and the sweet scent of flowers in the air. Monsoon days can be so cold they turn your lips blue, but soon enough, warm sunlight creeps back in, casting a soft glow outside your door. Sometimes your garden is alive with chirping birds and buzzing bees, and other times the trees bend wildly under the weight of a thunderstorm.

That's the rhythm of nature—the rhythm of life. You've got to listen to it, go with the flow, and not expect anything to be set in stone. Just be ready for whatever comes your way, whether it's a storm, a breakup, a small joy, a budding romance, or a surprise victory.

The key? Stay calm and welcome it all.

And here's some life advice: don't ever get too cocky. The universe (or God, if you prefer) isn't a fan of arrogance. So stay humble. Know your limits. Work hard, and whatever rewards come your way, welcome them with gratitude. If you can give to others, do it—there's no shortage of people out there who could use a helping hand. Giving is one of life's greatest comforts.

But don't overdo it—whether it's dieting, working, or even love, remember to pace yourself. What you lack in one area, life will often make up for in another.

If you're in a position to help someone, just do it. Don't expect anything in return— the universe has a way of sending the right people your way when you need them. It's one of life's little laws. So, take a deep breath, move with nature, and enjoy the dance.

143

## 64. WISHES AND MOMENTS

When we're young, we throw ourselves headfirst into life, chasing dreams and sparing no effort to make them come true. Some wishes pan out, but let's be honest—most don't. And sometimes, even when we finally get what we thought we wanted, it feels like nothing special after all. Before we know it, we're off chasing the next big thing, barely pausing to appreciate what we've already got.

Worse yet, in our relentless pursuit of new wishes, we breeze right past some of life's real treasures: a genuine friend, a deep love, a bit of truth, a golden opportunity, or even plain old good luck. All these precious things get left in the dust while we charge ahead, eyes locked on the next goal.

But here's the thing: an excellent hunter knows the value of patience. He doesn't rush. He waits, watches, and understands exactly when his quarry will appear. His real skill isn't in the chase—it's in the waiting. The bigger the prize, the more patience it demands.

Life's a lot like that. As you get older, you start to realize that patience is what really makes you wise. With time, you learn that everything has its perfect moment. You're on your way to your wishes, and whether you reach them today, tomorrow, or ten years from now, it's patience that will carry you there.

And along the way, you've got to respect whatever comes your way—whether it's happiness, sorrow, pain, failure, or even loss. All these moments are preparing you for the bigger picture. The best part? One day, your quarry might just wander right into your lap. But don't get too excited—sometimes the prize comes with its own set of headaches.

Since turning 50, I've taken up using prayer beads to remind myself of a few things: to be satisfied with what I have, to stop at the right time, and to follow my own rules. And when something *too* good comes my way, I remind myself to say, "How blissful!" three times—just to keep things in check.

## 65. DON'T BE A PATHETIC INFANTILE GUY

Every now and then, I hear my employees complain that a coworker played a dirty trick on them. Or my acquaintance will lament that he's just not a lucky person. Even my friend will admit he's lost more than a few things due to his own foolishness.

It's funny—deep down, we all want the same things: success, sincerity, kindness, a bit of pleasure, and affection. But here's the rub—the world doesn't exactly work like that. Success is this slippery thing, often judged by society's standards or through endless comparisons with others. And as for sincerity, kindness, pleasure, and affection? Well, they're beautiful words, but don't expect them to be showered upon you at every turn.

The truth is, success demands effort, persistence, and, let's be honest, a willingness to fight. Who do we fight? It's not just the people around us—it's ourselves. So, don't waste time waiting for someone to feel sorry for you or cut you a break. That's not how it works. If you're expecting a world full of compassion and endless pats on the back, you're setting yourself up for disappointment.

Even the most spiritually enlightened folks, those who've chosen to detach from worldly ambitions and focus on inner peace, have to fight for their awakening. No one's handing out comfort or shortcuts, not even in the spiritual realm.

The more success you're after, the more roadblocks life throws in your way. That's just the price of the game. Success is measured by how many hurdles you clear, not by how easy the path was.

So don't bother with all the endless comparisons—they're a waste of energy. Look inward, work on your own dignity, and aim for real growth.

And for heaven's sake, don't be that pathetic, immature guy who's stuck whining about how hard life is. I remind myself of that every day.

## 66. OBSERVE YOUR SELF-ADJUSTED PRECEPTS

The Buddha gave laypeople Five Precepts to live by, while monks have a whole laundry list of rules to follow—think of it like the difference between a casual yoga class and boot camp. But let's face it, modern life is way more complicated than life in a monastery, so we need to get creative with our precepts.

Now, precepts can feel as rigid as bricks fresh out of a factory mold—everything the same shape and size, no flexibility. But life? Life is more like a pile of mismatched stones. You need to take those uneven rocks and fit them together, let a rounded stone balance out a sharp one. With a little flexibility, you can build something solid without driving yourself crazy trying to make everything fit just right.

When we were young, we were basically wild animals. We went where we wanted, called any couch or floor "home," ate whatever we could find (sometimes even food), and didn't bother with rules. Fast forward to middle age, and suddenly we've got bad backs, grey hairs, and just enough wisdom to realize that maybe a little structure isn't such a bad idea after all. That's when it hits you: following some basic precepts is necessary to keep life from going completely off the rails.

So, I've come up with my own version of the Buddha's precepts. Think of them as "bricks and stones," with a little more give and take to keep things interesting. Here's my playbook:

**Basic Bricks:**

- No killing.

- No stealing.

- No hanky-panky.

**Basic Stones:**

- Stay away from killing anything bigger than a mosquito, and please—no encouraging your friends to be "big game hunters" either. At home, stick to fruits and veggies. If you're craving a steak, go out to eat but keep your kitchen free of animal casualties. And chew your food, for goodness' sake—show a little respect for what's on your plate.

146

- Never steal money or objects. But if you spot a good idea that isn't bolted down? Borrow away. (Just don't forget to sprinkle a little of your own creativity on it.)

- Keep things responsible. No flirting with trouble—and definitely no flirting with anyone who might have second thoughts. Treat people with kindness, but keep it above board.

So, there you have it—my personal set of precepts. It's all about balance, like turning life's endless rules into a game of Tetris where you can swap out some bricks for stones. The point is to live wisely, stay flexible, and not beat yourself up when things don't fit perfectly. Because let's be real: life rarely fits perfectly.

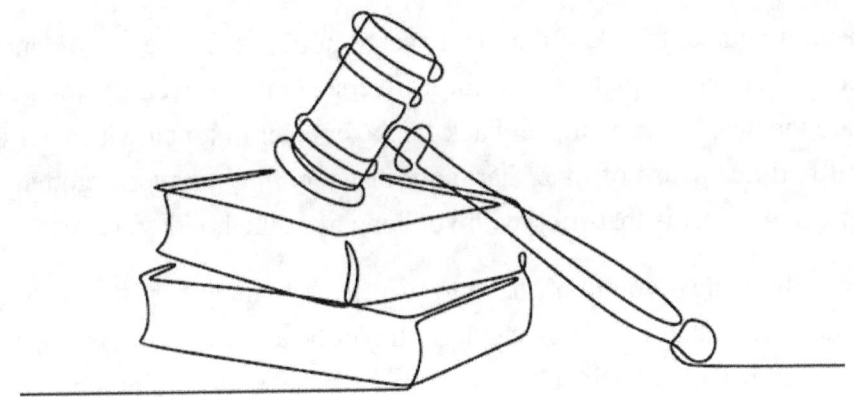

## 67. YOUR OWN FESTIVAL

There are plenty of big holidays every year, and let's not forget the minor ones sprinkled throughout the weeks—those built-in excuses to hit pause on your everyday worries and just kick back a little. These are the days when you get to hit refresh and live for yourself, even if just for a while.

So, ditch the boring looks and step out of your usual routine. Maybe spruce up your wardrobe, polish off those shoes you haven't worn in months, and grab a new bag or watch that makes you feel like a million bucks. Holidays are your chance to indulge a bit in the finer things—good meals, nice wine, and maybe even a night out with friends where the music is as good as the company (and maybe a few beautiful faces don't hurt either).

But holidays aren't just for stuffing your face and socializing. They give you time to slow down and focus on what really matters—like finally getting around to that concert you've been putting off or cooking a meal from scratch with love instead of out of habit. It's a chance to actually care for yourself or the ones you love in a way that goes beyond the everyday hustle.

And then, of course, there are the more sacred holidays. These are the moments to reflect on the bigger picture—on the Universe, God, or even just on yourself. These are the days when you peel back the layers, get in touch with your deeper self, and find that sense of inner harmony that you might have forgotten exists. These are the moments that stick with you long after the holiday passes.

But here's the thing—you don't have to wait for a holiday to roll around. Don't let the calendar dictate when you can have fun or be at peace. Turn every moment into your own personal festival. Celebrate life whenever you want—because why wait for a holiday to start enjoying it?

## 68. STRIPPING IT DOWN

### *Back to Basics*

Happiness, sorrow, fear, anger—on the surface, they all seem like different beasts. But at their core, they're the same species, just wearing different disguises. We get tangled up in them, expressing these emotions day after day, like we're starring in a soap opera that never ends. So, how do we make these pesky emotions disappear? How do we live without constantly chasing happiness or running from sorrow?

Most people spend their entire lives chasing that emotional high, believing happiness is something to be found outside themselves. But the Buddha? He flipped the script. He wasn't searching for happiness—he was looking for peace, that calm, emotionless state where you're not swinging from one feeling to the next like a human pendulum.

### *Staying Focused*

Steve Jobs hit the nail on the head: most of what we do in life is cluttered nonsense. We're busy creating mess after mess, and then we wonder why we're exhausted. The trick is to pick out the gems, focus on those, and let go of the rest. Just ditch the junk.

So here's my plan—starting now, I'm only going to write down the most noteworthy story of the day each evening. But let's be honest, even that story is just a leaf that's fallen from the tree—part of the bigger picture, but still just one small piece.

### *Simplify and Focus*

In a world where we chase emotions like kids chasing bubbles and create more clutter than we know what to do with, maybe the answer is simpler than we think. Strip it all down, focus on what matters, and let the rest fall away. Life doesn't have to be complicated—it just needs a little less noise and a lot more clarity.

## 69. COURAGE AND RESPONSIBILITY

Life's full of tough choices, and sooner or later, you're going to find yourself staring down a few forks in the road. Contradictory thoughts will circle like vultures, and you'll be the one left to make the call. Some decisions will be easy, but many will be the kind that make you lose sleep and reach for the ice cream.

When you're young, it's a different ball game. You charge forward fearlessly, ready to take on the world. Decisions? You make them with passion, owning them, right or wrong. Sure, sometimes you stumble, but you're always eager and fired up. You've got that clarity of youth, and the road ahead seems wide open.

But then you get older. And with experience and success come more voices in your ear. Suddenly, every decision feels like it's weighed down by a committee of advisors. You hesitate, take longer to decide, and before you know it, creativity starts to take a back seat. Gone are the bold, impressive results of your younger days. Now, it's all about playing it safe.

But here's what I've learned: more often than not, the decision you make on your own, without all the second-guessing and outside input, is the one that's truest to you. So, trust yourself. Have the guts to make the final call, be brave about it, and stick to it, whether it's about work, life, or just what to eat for dinner.

And here's the kicker: sometimes, you've got to say "no." Sometimes, circumstances change, and you need to pivot. Don't overthink it—just make the call and move on. Own your decisions and take responsibility for wherever they lead you.

Life is constantly flowing, and what worked today may be history tomorrow. You need the courage to evolve, even if it means tearing down what you built yesterday to make room for tomorrow's opportunities.

Of course, listen to advice, take other people's opinions into account, but at the end of the day, the decision is yours—whether it's brilliant or a total flop.

So, pluck up your courage and make the call. After all, life's too short to wait for everyone's approval.

## 70. TEMPORARY HAPPINESS

Honestly, I have no idea what happiness really is. Is it a feeling or some elusive state of being? It seems like happiness is tied to checking off a wish list: accomplishing something after countless obstacles, making money, snagging something you love, meeting "the one," having great sex, finding your soulmate, getting that promotion, or even winning a little fame.

But here's the catch—all of that takes a *lot* of effort. The road to happiness is usually paved with potholes, unexpected detours, and moments of "why did I even start this?" Before you get to the good stuff, you've got to trudge through the muck of sorrow, frustration, and general unhappiness. It's like the universe saying, "You want happiness? Prove it."

So, yeah—happiness is a fleeting state of mind, and let's face it, unhappiness shows up way more often. And then one day, it hits you: most of our happy (or unhappy) moments are tied to someone else. We end up comparing our happiness to theirs, which makes it even more fragile.

Happiness depends on others or things outside of us, which makes it as delicate as a soap bubble. It doesn't last long, but we chase after it anyway. It's like planting a flower—it takes forever for it to grow, and when it finally blooms, the joy only lasts a few days (or sometimes just a few hours) before the flower wilts. Meanwhile, the process of getting it there? It's *long* and exhausting.

Ideally, we want the plant to grow and blossom without needing constant attention—just bloom already! But, of course, it doesn't work that way. Even wildflowers, which bloom without our help, fade quickly. Still, they're beautiful while they last, and that brief beauty makes the effort worth it.

Sure, happiness is temporary. But hey, it's better to have a little happiness now and then than to be stuck with nothing but gloom. After all, a few good flowers are better than none.

# 71. MAKING LOVE IS AN ART FORM

Let's face it—making love almost always ends in some form of sadness. It could be a vague, fleeting sadness, the kind that leaves you feeling a little lost, empty, or just plain sleepy.

Making love is also about loss. Each time, it seems to chip away a bit of your desire, your connection, or at least some of that mysterious life force that keeps things spicy.

It's no wonder that making love is often compared to art—because like art, it takes effort, skill, and a bit of finesse. Think of it like taming a wild animal or breaking in a horse. It's no easy feat. It's more like crossing a perilous mountain pass or walking across a narrow bridge over a deep chasm.

And that climax everyone's always talking about? Well, that's like reaching the peak without losing your footing. You've got to help your partner hit O-land without losing your own strength in the process. Picture this: you and your horse (metaphorically speaking) reach the top of the mountain together. The horse rears up, neighs triumphantly, and you're still firmly in the saddle. If you've done it right, you and your horse can continue on, conquering several more mountains together.

Timing is everything. If you and your horse don't hit the peak together, you're going to find yourself exhausted at the base of the mountain, thinking you've made it to the top when, really, you've barely started. And if you're not careful, one day your horse might leave you for a better rider!

So, what's the secret? You've got to move with the terrain. Walk steadily on the ascent, pick up speed when you're on level ground, stay sharp during the tricky parts, and take your time when the road is rough. Know when to move forward and when to pull back. Never be careless. It might seem like you're only aiming for a few minutes (or even seconds) of bliss, but the preparation should take hours.

As the old saying goes, a great rider always has a loyal horse. But let's be real— sometimes even the best riders spare their favorite horse and borrow a temporary one for those longer, more grueling journeys.

## 72. UNLUCKY

I've had my fair share of bad luck—missed opportunities, wrong turns, and just flat-out unfortunate events. My colleagues often blame their own failures on bad luck too. They figure it's just the universe playing a cruel joke, dropping misfortune on them out of nowhere, while others with seemingly less talent cruise through life without a hitch.

But here's the deal: life is like an unpredictable ocean. Sometimes it's calm, sometimes it's rough, and sometimes it's just waiting for the perfect moment to knock you off your feet. Everything around you looks a little suspicious if you stare at it long enough. It's like life has this lurking sense of danger, just waiting for the right moment to trip you up. And that's the thing—danger is a part of the package.

If everything were smooth sailing and success came easy, the world would be overrun with arrogant, self-satisfied people. And let's be honest, that would be boring. Who wants to live in a world where everyone's puffed up with pride? Not me.

So, what can you do? Stay alert. Life has a funny way of throwing curveballs when you least expect them, and you've got to be ready. Sure, it might feel like the rug gets pulled out from under you, but don't turn and run. Stand your ground, even when tension is high and confusion is swirling around. The secret is endurance and patience. It's the only way to keep moving forward and protect yourself from life's sucker punches.

And if you fail? Well, remind yourself that you gave it your best shot. You were brave, you faced it head-on, and sometimes things just go beyond what we can handle. Accept it, learn from it, and know that sometimes, being unlucky is just part of the ride.

## 73. MOUNTAIN TOPS AND FORESTS

We conquered the highest mountain in the early morning, trekking through the untouched jungle under a blanket of stars. We trudged through endless green forests, scaled cliffs, and splashed across streams and waterfalls. We even slogged through sticky mud—because of course, nature loves to throw in a little extra challenge.

When we finally reached the top, the sun was just starting to stretch its rays into every corner, and we let out triumphant shouts. All around us, there was nothing but fog-covered peaks and forests stretching as far as the eye could see. We might have crossed some of those very mountains and forests on our journey up here. But at that moment, we felt on top of the world.

And yet, like most victories, the glorious happiness on the mountain top was fleeting. Soon enough, it was time to head back down, through the same wild forests, swamps, and brooks. The wilderness, with all its mysteries and hidden dangers, was waiting for us again—just as unknown as before. We rushed down through other, smaller mountains, eager to get home, forgetting that it's not just about reaching the peak but also about how we handle the descent.

The truth is, the forest has been standing there for centuries. It stands tall through sunlight, rain, and fog, protecting secrets and hidden trails to the mountain top. The mountain might give you that glorious high, but the forest? That's where the real adventure happens.

Climbing high mountains tests your willpower. It pushes you to unlock your potential and forces you to recognize the hidden traps along the way. But entering the forest—that's where you truly learn.

Most of the time, you'll walk through life's challenges alone, but every now and then, a companion shows up and gives you a little extra strength when you need it. And don't forget—this civilized, urban jungle we call home? It's just another forest, full of undiscovered peaks waiting for you to conquer.

## 74. ALWAYS BE READY

The world is in a constant state of flux—sometimes things get better, sometimes worse, and then there are those times when everything feels stuck, like you're wading through a swamp.

In the midst of it all, we like to think we've got it figured out. Maybe we're doing what we love or feel like we're shaping our own little corner of the universe. Back in our youth, we were always ready for whatever came our way—whether it was a new adventure, a romantic escapade, or an attempt at world domination (or at least a decent road trip).

But then one day, reality smacks us in the face. We realize that we're not really in control of anything and that we're more fragile and delusional than we care to admit. All we've been doing is riding the waves of life and reacting to whatever pops up next. It turns out, life's a bit like that unpredictable ocean we keep hearing about—it's unstable, unclear, and just when you think you've got it mastered, a rogue wave knocks you off your feet.

Now, society is constantly shifting—one or two revolutions are always bubbling up somewhere. Even when it feels like nothing's happening, there's always an undercurrent of change moving things along.

When will things shift? What's coming next? Where will it happen? And who's involved? We have no clue. The trick is to stay sharp, observe, wait for it, and always be ready—because in the end, it's all a guessing game.

By the time I reached the autumn of my life, I realized there's really only one thing we can be sure of: death is certain. Someday, we're all going to punch that ticket. Knowing this, I've stopped rushing through life. Instead, I work at a steady pace, enjoy every moment I have, and make sure I'm as prepared as I can be for whatever comes next.

That's what crossed my mind while waiting for the traffic lights to turn green at the crossroads. Long lines of cars surrounded me, horns blaring, the morning sun shining brightly. A new day was beginning—whether I was ready for it or not.

## 75. DELICATE AND PROFOUND

I've met some delicate and sensitive folks in my time—people who seem to pick up on every glance, smile, or gesture around them. With a flick of dust off your collar or a reassuring arm around your shoulder, they have a way of easing your worries and making you feel like everything's going to be okay. But here's the thing: sometimes they're about as deep as a kiddie pool. You think you've found a kindred spirit, but really, you've just gotten cozy with a face, a pose, or a habit. They breeze past you, and before you know it, you realize there's not much substance there.

On the flip side, I've also crossed paths with some deeply profound and intelligent people—the kind who can unravel the most complicated issues like they're solving a crossword puzzle. But they come with their quirks. They can be haughty, looking down on you with an almost holy silence. And don't get me started on their appearance. They might sport thick glasses that practically scream "genius," let their nose hair roam free, and could care less about their teeth. They might even stroll around town in slippers like they're too smart to bother with shoes. Let's just say, their intelligence doesn't always translate into style.

Sometimes, you hope for some wise counsel or at least a pearl of wisdom from these profound minds. But instead, you get something that smells suspiciously like their mental garbage.

Then, there are the rare ones—those who are both subtle and profound. They tend to keep a low profile, having been through enough failures to make them quiet and contemplative. They don't say much, but when they do, it's worth listening to. They move through life slowly, carefully, and with attention to detail. They're simple but profound in every gesture, living not just for themselves but enriching the world around them in the process.

Being around them brings a certain peace, the kind that feels like you've stumbled upon something precious.

Live your life like that—quietly brilliant, a little subtle, a lot profound—and you'll find that peace of enlightenment for yourself.

## 76. FRAGILE EMOTIONS

Sadness, love, hatred, misery, happiness—they're all just part of the emotional roller coaster we call life. Emotions tend to show up when we reach a tipping point or wrap up something that's drained our brain or body.

When you stir up someone's emotions, you're setting them on a new path. You might surprise them, make them feel alive, or even send them into a bit of an emotional frenzy. That's the magic of emotions—they're what make us human.

Now, humans like to think we're rational beings. And sure, we can be—when we're not being steered by our feelings. But let's be real: emotions are the fuel behind most of our behaviors. And they're as unpredictable as a candle in the wind. One moment, they're burning bright, and the next, they're flickering out. That's why human behavior is such a wild card.

A good leader knows how to tap into people's emotions. When a group shares the same feeling, the leader gains an incredible power to influence them. And that power? It can either build something great or burn it all down.

We see it all the time—positive emotions like hope or love inspire people to do good. But negative emotions like anger or jealousy? They push people toward some pretty regrettable choices. And yet, life isn't always that simple. Sometimes, enthusiasm can go too far and cross dangerous lines, while something as negative as feeling inferior can light a fire of determination that drives a person to greatness.

So yeah, emotions are tricky to explain.

The people who know how to manipulate emotions are either experienced pros or, let's be honest, a little bit cunning. And the ones who wear their hearts on their sleeves? Those are the sincere folks—the ones who may get labeled as naive or even a bit foolish by society.

But here's the thing: it's up to you. You can choose to be the sincere one, or you can lean into your crafty side. Just know, both paths come with their own set of challenges.

## 77. HEALTH

When we think about health, it's usually about not being sick and maybe squeezing in some exercise or sports. And sure, that's a good start—but it's only part of the picture. We're more than just bodies. We've got hearts, minds, and spirits to look after too.

So, beyond just hitting the gym to dodge illness, you've got to work out your mind—read, learn something new every day, admire a sunset, or find those little moments that make your heart dance. And don't forget to nurture your spirit—spend time exploring whatever faith or sense of wonder you have about this big, mysterious universe and dig into the secrets hiding inside of you.

Modern life pretty much hands you everything on a silver platter. You want to exercise? There's a fitness center on every corner. Need to stir up some emotion? Hit the theater, visit a museum, or even grab a drink at a bar. Want to expand your mind? Go to school, hit the library, or just dive into life and see what lessons it throws at you. And when it comes to faith, well, monasteries, churches, and places of worship are always ready to welcome you in.

But here's the catch: all that stuff? It's external. It's what the world gives you to help measure how far you've come. And, honestly, I'm not buying it.

When you're young, sure, you reflect and think deeply about life. You practice, stumble, and adjust as you go. But as you get older, you realize that the real work isn't about what's out there—it's about what's going on inside. You stop seeking answers in the world and start looking for them within yourself. You observe, stumble into your own thoughts, and find your way by going inward.

You don't have to go anywhere special. Turn your home into your own monastery, your own sacred space. Take care of it. Serve it. Respect it. Because at the end of the day, the best place to find balance, health, and peace is right where you are.

## 78. KNOWLEDGE IS NOT ENOUGH

You spend years building up your knowledge—first in school, then in life. What you learn in school gets tested and reshaped by the real world, and what you pick up in life helps fill in the gaps that school missed. You think you're getting somewhere. Sometimes you even succeed. But, let's be honest, most of the time, you trip, stumble, and faceplant right into failure. You dust yourself off, get back up, and keep going, like a boxer squaring off against life itself.

But here's the kicker: intelligence, experience, and knowledge? Not enough. They're just part of the equation in this never-ending match. You've also got to master resilience, learn to forgive yourself, and endure whatever life throws at you. You've got to get comfortable with stepping back, sometimes in shame, sometimes being overlooked or forgotten.

And guess what? That's still not enough.

At some point, you'll hit a wall and think, "Maybe I need a little something extra." That's when you find yourself in the strange world of shamans and rituals. Maybe they'll read the stars, interpret the wind, or offer some mysterious insight that makes you feel better, even if you don't quite understand why. You walk away feeling a bit more secure, even though the future is still a big question mark. You can't say why you won or lost, but now you're convinced it might just be about luck.

There's something about life that we just don't know. It's not written in books or explained in classes. It's something tied to the stars, to luck, to relationships, to the strange brew of experiences you've accumulated along the way. It's something that belongs to you alone, something that comes from deep within.

So, yeah—knowledge is great, but it's never enough. Life is a bit more of a mystery than that. Just think about it.

# 79. THE PATH FROM MISERY TO HAPPINESS

## Say Thanks to Misery

We all know that loneliness, worry, and sorrow come knocking far too often. No matter how good you are at handling life's curveballs, sometimes you hit a home run, and other times, you strike out. The highs are great, but they're short-lived, and before you know it, you're back to square one, dealing with the same old feelings.

As you grow older, you start to realize something important: joy doesn't stick around forever, and frankly, you don't want to go back to feeling unhappy either. What you begin craving isn't another high but a steady, peaceful mind and a life that's calm, even in its simplicity.

Oddly enough, it's not happiness but misery that pushes you toward finding that peace. Misery has a way of nudging you to seek something more lasting and real. So, next time you're feeling down, don't just pray for peace—say thanks to misery for leading you there in the first place.

## Searching Means Happiness

Ever notice how the busiest times in life are often when we feel the happiest? We're all on a mission to find happiness, but oddly, it's the search itself that seems to bring us the most joy.

Tidying up the house, cooking a great meal, catching up with friends, or exploring new places—it's the movement, the change, that makes us feel alive. Sure, peaceful days are nice, but they can get boring after a while. We're wired to chase after something new, even if we don't quite know what it is.

As Tagore wisely said: *The many rough years, at great expense,*

*Journeying through many countries,*

*I went to see high mountains,*

*I went to see oceans,*

*Only I had not seen,*

*At my own doorstep,*

*The dew drops glistening on the ear of corn.*

Sometimes we search the world for happiness when it's been quietly waiting for us at home all along. But that's the beauty of the chase—it's what keeps us going.

## A Game of Luck

Remember Robinson Crusoe? Stranded on a deserted island, at first he felt like life had dealt him the worst hand possible. But after the initial panic, he calmed down and looked at his situation more carefully.

*"Bad luck,"* he thought. But then he realized, *"Wait, I'm still alive. That's good luck."* Sure, he was stuck in misery, but at least he wasn't floating dead in the ocean.

It's all about perspective. Crusoe could have focused on what he didn't have—no clothes, no comfort—but instead, he made the best of it. He was stranded, sure, but at least the weather was warm enough that he didn't need clothes!

There's a fine line between good luck and bad luck, and the trick is to walk it with optimism. Positive thinking is more useful than we give it credit for.

## The Balance of Life

Life is a constant interplay between misery, the search for happiness, and a game of luck. Misery pushes us to find peace, the search itself brings moments of joy, and luck—well, it's all in how you look at it. Happiness, as fleeting as it may be, is worth chasing, and peace, as elusive as it seems, is waiting for us when we stop and listen. The trick is to see the good even in bad times and to recognize that the journey itself is where much of the magic happens.

## 80. MISPERCEPTIONS

We get so much wrong in life. The funny thing is, we all know that everything is temporary. It's not exactly a secret—people have been talking about it for ages. Yet here we are, constantly hustling for money, chasing after fame and power, seeking out new experiences, and sometimes even indulging in things we shouldn't. We're in such a rush to get more that we rarely stop to enjoy what we already have.

I've seen people work themselves into an early grave, thinking they were climbing the ladder to success, only to realize too late that no one even remembers their name a few weeks after the funeral. Ministers, CEOs, influencers—you name it. Once they're gone, it's like they never existed.

Nothing lasts after death.

We're so caught up in making a living that we forget we're also heading toward the end of that life, without ever stopping to ask why we're here in the first place. What's our purpose? Why are we running this race when the finish line doesn't even come with a prize?

Here's the kicker: we're always trying to get more, without realizing that every gain comes with a cost. The older we get, the more entangled we become in our bonds—to people, to things, to ideas. Life becomes a balancing act between all these ties we've created. But when the final curtain falls, those bonds disappear, leaving us wondering why we got so wrapped up in them in the first place.

Everything changes. Nothing is permanent. Possessions come and go. Our lives are like drops of water that form, evaporate, and disappear into the air. The only thing that's real is the present moment—and our endless concerns about what's next. So maybe it's time to let go of the misperceptions and just live.

## 81. WHY THE RUSH?

We always seem to be in a rush. Rushing to do something, get somewhere, meet someone, eat a meal, make love, say goodbye. Even our thoughts are in a hurry—chasing after some idea that may not even be real. And in the end, we're hurrying toward the one thing we really shouldn't be so eager to meet: Death.

Being hasty doesn't make us more productive; if anything, it does the opposite. We end up doing a half-hearted job because while we're working on one thing, our minds are already on to the next. We're constantly being pulled in different directions, so we're never fully present. It's like we're passengers on a train, always running to catch the last one but never quite making it. And if by chance we do hop on, we spend the whole ride thinking about the next stop.

Life passes us by while we're busy daydreaming or overthinking. We're driven by the outside world's endless demands—always in a rush to get somewhere or achieve something. But our hasty wishes often lead to failed plans, with new temptations waiting just around the corner, ready to distract us all over again.

Honestly, I don't know what's going on in the minds of "successful" people. Maybe they feel pretty lonely up there at the top. They're always pushing forward, needing to be number one, the leader, the richest, the best. Social titles are like shiny bait they can't resist, and they chase after them in a never-ending race.

But here's the kicker: we all die, whether we're at the top or the bottom. All the success we're so eager to grab? We leave it all behind anyway.

So, why the rush? Slow down. Take care of yourself. Life isn't going anywhere.

## 82. A LOOK AT MYSELF

I had just returned from a golf party when a thought struck me:

Those in power who possess genuine talent and know how to carry themselves always seem to have a circle of friends, even when retirement comes calling. They know who'll still be around to shoot the breeze with them when they've reached that leisurely age.

Then there are those in power who, while sharp and clever enough to rise through the ranks, never quite grasp the art of behaving well. When they step down, they find themselves lonelier than expected.

And let's not forget the shameless and domineering types. No matter how many years roll by, no matter how life nudges them with lessons, they remain the same—shameless in anything they do, anywhere, anytime.

And what about the women—graceful and talented—who must navigate rooms full of loud voices and inflated egos? They're like flowers that bring beauty to a garden but are often surrounded by swarms. It's not always easy, but sometimes that's the reality of the world they must move through.

When we look at people—whether they're in power or striving to stay afloat, humble or cunning, brash or struggling, graceful or skilled—it eventually feels like nothingness. Life's grand stage spins on, never quite circling back. The outer trappings—whether titles, money, or admiration—are like jewelry: shiny but temporary. The only thing that endures is our own understanding of it all.

So, I think it's worth sitting down with ourselves now and then, taking a breather from the things we can't control. Let's focus on what truly matters—knowing that each moment we're in is all we really have, and that's where the real value lies.

## 83. LIFE DESIRES

There is one desire that always exists in your life. When you were young, you threw yourself into work. You barely had time for proper meals, grabbing whatever you could, and drinking anything that came your way. If you got drunk, it wasn't because the wine tasted good—it was either for the party or to numb your pain. Back then, you wanted to make lots of money and become famous overnight. And so, you became prey to all kinds of desires: impulsiveness, arrogance, loneliness, and lust. These desires followed you, controlled you. It became hard to distinguish between hunger and satisfaction, deprivation and enjoyment, using and enjoying.

As time passed, you realized you didn't have the strength to satisfy all those desires. You began to understand that you needed to step away from the excesses— less alcohol, less meat, more vegetables and fruit. You told yourself to live in moderation, to stop ogling beautiful women, and if they ever came near, to treat them as you would anyone else.

You started to find balance and harmony. You thought you could control yourself. You became quieter; your desires seemed to cool off. You moved like a zoo animal, ambling leisurely through life, sometimes roaring suddenly with a flash of instinct.

But you were wrong.

Like the human body, which is built with perfect balance and harmony, everything comes in symmetrical pairs. If a body part appears singularly, it sits in the center. However, there is one organ that rests off to the side. It's always pumping, always keeping you alive.

Desire lies in your heart. It is the drive behind your life. Live in accordance with your true needs and your unique personality.

## 84. JUST GIVE AND FORGET IT

The Buddha hit the nail on the head when he said that all suffering comes from greed, anger, and ignorance. Now, I may not be the best interpreter of his teachings, but here's my take.

Think about a kid. He's always demanding something—a toy, a hug, new clothes. And if he doesn't get what he wants, cue the waterworks and sulking. Then he grows up, and it doesn't get much better. He starts comparing himself to others, trying to keep up with the Joneses. Eventually, as an adult, his whole life's focus becomes about trading: efforts for money, emotions for favors, and kindness for future benefits. Relationships become this two-way street where everyone's keeping score, trading one thing for another.

But here's the kicker—this kind of mindset only fuels greed. The more we get, the more we want. And it never stops. The new car gets old, the new phone's outdated in a year, and we're constantly chasing the next best thing. Before long, disappointment and anger creep in when life doesn't measure up to our endless demands. That's where ignorance and anger start growing like weeds.

The Buddha, wise as ever, offered a solution: live simply, like a hermit or a monk, and want for nothing. Easy, right? Well, maybe not for those of us still in the grind of daily life. I mean, we've got bills to pay and responsibilities to juggle.

But here's something I've learned since hitting 50: there's a way to live without getting sucked into the greed trap. Give—give your time, your effort, your care—without expecting anything in return. And you know what? The universe has a funny way of rewarding you in unexpected ways when you least expect it.

So, stop overthinking it. Just give and forget it. The rest will take care of itself.

# Part III
# REALM OF HUMANS

*On this endless journey, with no clear destination in sight,*

*I've traveled to countless places, seen a million things—*

*Tasted victory, swallowed defeat, felt joy and sadness,*

*Gained and lost more than I could ever count.*

*Things come and go like they always do, naturally and effortlessly.*

*But the feelings linger, don't they? Those deep, quiet echoes inside us.*

*The happiness we borrow eventually returns to its rightful owner.*

*And as I keep moving toward that elusive place with no name,*

*I realize—it's not the destination that matters after all.*

## 1. THE JOURNEY OF LIFE

In Buddhism, the three treasures are Buddha, Dharma, and Sangha. In life, we each have our own trio of essentials:

- **Relationships**: the art of not strangling each other while coexisting

- **Methods**: the rules we create to run the chaotic carnival called society

- **The Truth**: that elusive thing hiding behind everything and everyone

And on your own pilgrimage through life, you pass through three stages:

**1. The Child Becomes the Traveler**: You start off wide-eyed and carefree, but soon enough, you're hauling around a heavy suitcase full of responsibilities, ambitions, disappointments, hopes, and sorrows. You trudge along for decades, picking up more baggage along the way.

**2. The Traveler Becomes the Wise Man**: After miles of wandering, you finally figure out what's worth carrying and what's not. You lighten the load, leave some things by the roadside, and walk with a spring in your step again. You begin to accept life as it is—flaws and all.

**3. The Wise Man Becomes Childlike**: Eventually, you circle back to where you started—seeing the world through childlike eyes again. You welcome life as it comes, live in harmony with the universe, and find peace in simplicity. You've returned to a state of pure freedom.

And finally, when the time comes, you'll be free to return to the dust and ashes from where you began—with no baggage at all.

## 2. MORALITY

People love talking about morality—on TV, on the radio, in newspapers. Everyone has a soapbox, whether they're philosophers, politicians, judges, teachers, spouses, or parents.

But what is morality, really? Does it mean:

No corruption, no materialism, no stepping on the little guy, no adultery, no sneaky daydreams about someone else's spouse, no stealing, no funny business, no greed, no waste, and no lies?

That sounds great on paper, but let's be real—everyone's chasing *money, love, and fame*. These are life's big shiny carrots, and we spend our days running after them, trying to collect as much as we can.

So, how does anyone hold on to their morality while chasing after all these worldly prizes? Even if you pretend you're above it all, deep down, those desires are always lurking, ready to pop up. You can't fool yourself forever.

Living a moral life, then, isn't about pretending you're free from all temptation. It's about learning to reconcile with those inner desires—knowing when enough is enough, letting go before things spiral out of control. It's about calming the racing heart, taking deep breaths, and not sneaking around in fear of getting caught by your conscience, the Almighty, or worse—your own guilt.

## 3. NIRVANA AND HELL

The world is packed with unwanted surprises—misery lurking at every corner, waiting to trip us up. Naturally, the idea of escaping all that suffering sounds pretty good. Somewhere far away, full of peace and joy, sounds like paradise.

That's called Nirvana. But here's the catch: nobody really knows where it is.

You'll hear all sorts of vague descriptions—think travel brochures written by monks. But only the Buddha and a few enlightened souls, the Arhats, seem to have a real sense of direction. They're happy to point out the path, but don't expect a personal escort. This is a solo trip.

Getting there is no weekend getaway, either. It's a marathon that stretches across lifetimes, full of reincarnations, dead ends, and more spiritual hurdles than you'd ever expect.

There's no shortcut. As Buddha laid it out, live your life full of greed, grudges, jealousy—or on the flip side, chasing pleasures and riding waves of anger—and you're basically turning your life into a do-it-yourself version of hell. On the other hand, if you live like a monk, cutting off your desires and isolating yourself from all temptations, congratulations—you're getting closer to Nirvana.

Too much desire? Welcome to hell.

A life without any? That's Nirvana.

It's not easy, that's for sure.

The choice is yours. But, is there some third path—a cozy middle ground between Nirvana and hell? Maybe, just maybe, there's a way to balance the two.

# 4. BODY

This body of ours—it's a real double-edged sword. On one side, it brings us a lot of joy, letting us experience the world through all kinds of sensual delights that light up our emotions like a neon sign. On the other side, it's responsible for some pretty regrettable moments, when those same senses run wild and we lose control. Not to mention, it's a constant source of trouble when it decides to get sick.

To keep from getting too caught up in life's fleeting pleasures, the Buddha had some handy advice: think of the body like a skin bag. Inside? Bones, muscles, organs, and all sorts of unmentionable fluids. Sounds gross, right? But it's the truth.

So, the next time a beautiful person catches your eye and stirs up some not-so-noble thoughts, just picture that skin bag full of goo, and—voila!—your lust will vanish faster than a disappearing act in Vegas.

Feeling a little too full of yourself? Remind yourself that, one day, this same body will be buried deep underground, decomposing like last week's leftovers. Arrogance doesn't stand a chance.

The Buddha also compared the *body to a musical instrument*. Tighten the strings too much, and the sound is unbearable. Too loose, and it won't play a note. But with just the right tension, a skilled player can make beautiful music.

So, what was the Buddha getting at? Well, it's all about finding the right balance—whether you're tightening or loosening your "strings," it all depends on the situation.

I guess it's time for me to *learn how to tune this instrument* of mine a little better.

## 5. POLITENESS

Ah, the world—what a perplexing place. We're constantly taught to be proper, polite, and well-behaved. But then, the very things about girls that are meant to be subtle and graceful—like their clothes, their posture, and their style—ironically draw all the attention.

As gentlemen, we're told we shouldn't glance at that tempting belly button peeking out beneath a short T-shirt. Nor should we let our gaze wander to those silky thighs beneath a super-short skirt or get caught staring at the ample curves behind a low-cut blouse.

So, what are we supposed to look at? Quite the riddle, right? Maybe the eyes! Yes, the eyes—always the safest bet. And if your mischievous eyes start betraying you, tempted to roam where they shouldn't, just close them and nod along to whatever story she's telling. You might not know what she's saying, but trust me, it'll score you major points.

Politeness never looked so smooth.

175

# 6. PLEASURE AND PAIN

As humans, we are marvelously complex creatures—endowed with both a heart to relish pleasure and a brain to explore the world while training our will. This duality is why we possess the unique ability to create and destroy, love and despair, all in a single lifetime.

Now, take animals, for example. They've got it easy! They find joy in the simple things—eating, mating, playing. Sure, they might work now and then, but the minute they're done, they go right back to lounging without a care in the world. They live in harmony with nature's rhythms, never overthinking, never worrying about tomorrow's to-do list. But, alas, no cow grazing in a field of grass ever woke up one day and achieved enlightenment. A cow's journey from lunch to dinner doesn't exactly leave room for spiritual breakthroughs.

Only humans, who can wrestle with life's complexities and cultivate a spiritual life, have a shot at becoming something more—a Buddha perhaps! But let's not sugarcoat it—it's a tough gig.

As humans, we're wired to chase after pleasure. But here's the catch: we also know, deep down, that chasing after those pleasures often brings pain along for the ride. More pleasure equals more pain—it's like the universe's cruel joke. The more you cling to fleeting joy, the more you suffer when it's gone.

So, what's the solution? Well, the spiritual journey is all about this:

1. Waive those fleeting pleasures.

2. Live like an ox in chastity (minus the grazing, of course).

3. Get serious about meditation and train your mind.

4. And, who knows? You might just find yourself reaching that enlightened state of Buddha-like calm.

It's a tall order, but then again, no one ever said becoming a Buddha was easy.

## 7. SINS

Sins have a funny way of catching up with us, whether through the legal system, the judgmental eyes of society, or, worst of all, our own relentless conscience. It's as if karma has a better memory than we do.

Now, if you happen to realize your wrongdoing and feel a pang of regret, there's hope. You might just get a lighter sentence—or at least sleep a little easier at night. But here's the tricky part: sometimes, we don't even know we've sinned. The line between right and wrong can be as wobbly as a drunk trying to walk a straight line. It shifts depending on who's involved, what's happening, and the angle you look at it from.

Occasionally, sins sneak up on us, born out of good intentions but delivering unintended consequences. And let's be honest, most sins are rooted in the mind. So, who can we turn to when our internal compass starts spinning wildly?

Truth? Well, that's a moving target—changing with the times like fashion trends or political winds.

At the end of the day, if a sinner remains in the dark, even when they're muttering "I'm sorry" and feeling all repentant, there's little hope unless they stumble across a wise mentor. Enter Buddha, stage left. With a guide like that, even the worst of us—a murderer, a thief, or a world-weary soul—can find redemption and, dare I say, enlightenment.

As for me, I like to think I'm a decent person with a compassionate heart. Now, where do I sign up to find my own awakened mentor?

## 8. MIND

You wear many hats in life, don't you? Depending on the moment, you might be the sweet, caring friend or the firm, no-nonsense boss. Sometimes you're the angel bringing comfort, and other times, well, you let your inner devil out for a little fun. It's funny how our personalities work like a kaleidoscope, constantly shifting and showing different sides of who we are.

The mind is no different—it's like a wild universe all on its own. Thoughts race around like kids on a sugar high, bumping into each other, scattering across different levels of consciousness. One minute, your mind might be a greedy little creature, pulling at every desire. Then, without warning, it floats to some heavenly place full of peace and light. And sometimes it's just plain lost in the dark, stewing in anger or swirling with joy, or even reaching moments of calm wisdom.

What's wild is you don't need to wait for death to experience new lives or realms. Right there in your mind, you've got it all: hungry ghosts, moments of heavenly bliss, dumb animals wandering aimlessly, fierce warriors, and even the peace of Nirvana.

So, here's the thing—you get to choose where you spend your time. It's all within you.

## 9. THE PRICE OF GREATNESS

The lives of some great men seem like a parade of strange surprises, don't they? You have a composer who gifted the world with timeless masterpieces, all while indulging in a same-sex relationship that society wasn't ready for. Or that old poet whose noble verses took your breath away, yet he lost his head over an innocent young woman. And let's not forget the brilliant philosopher, writing pages of wisdom while syphilis slowly claimed him.

These folks are like towering trees, their branches stretching skyward, but their roots? Deep in the dark, messy soil of life. And maybe that's the deal—those roots need to dig into something raw, something mysterious, to draw the energy that fuels greatness.

Is it any different in today's world? The higher a person climbs in society, the more tangled they get in factions, alliances, and power plays. The wealthier they become, the trickier their dealings are. It's almost as if brilliance comes at a cost.

And look at some of the finest writing—often born out of poverty, like a well dug deep enough to pull up the sweetest, purest water. You can't predict it. Maybe the struggles are part of the price you pay for creating something extraordinary.

# 10. CHOICE

Each of us is heading toward the same inevitable fate—death—and along the way, we wrestle with the big questions: Will everything end? Is there something after death? And perhaps most importantly, what should we do while we're still breathing?

Everyone has their own take on these questions, but generally, life seems to offer us three main lifestyle choices:

*1. Enjoyment*: Ah, the sweet life. Enjoyment brings us joy, no doubt, but also its fair share of pain. Plus, if you're not careful, it can lead you into a lazy spiral of indulgence where you can get stuck chasing the next good time.

*2. Creativity*: Now, this one's all about discovery and putting something new into the world. But make no mistake—it's hard work. Creativity doesn't come easy. It's born from sleepless nights, endless trial and error, and a lot of elbow grease.

*3. Virtue*: Virtue—noble, upright, and... honestly, kind of boring. Precepts and teachings? Not exactly a wild ride. But virtue keeps us grounded, even when it feels like a grind.

Most religions would tell you that virtue is the way to go. Yet plenty of people live their lives fueled by enjoyment or creativity and still sleep well at night. Half the world doesn't subscribe to any religion at all—they live for pleasure or creativity, but sooner or later, even the most carefree among us might feel the tug toward something more virtuous.

The gold standard, they say, is balancing all three—enjoyment, creativity, and virtue. But let's be honest, balance isn't easy. Life tends to rip us in different directions, caught between contradictions and conflicts.

Maybe the trick is to rotate them—creativity in the morning, enjoyment in the afternoon, and virtue by bedtime. Or mix it up: perhaps a little indulgence at night, a creative spark when the sun rises, and a sprinkle of virtue in between. There's no one-size-fits-all because life is a buffet, not a set menu.

Choices, choices. Fortunately, life's diversity keeps things interesting.

## 11. LETTING GO AND WAITING

### *Waiting*

*Do you bring anything, Tomorrow?*

*Or is it just the same road and a steady stream of people?*

*The night falls, the streets grow empty, flickering with dim lights.*

*Conference by conference, year by year—they all blur together.*

*The row of trees still stands by the street,*

*Witnessing the endless parade of life's comings and goings.*

*So many plans, so many schemes—what's left behind in the dust?*

*Why do we cling so tightly?*

*Why not just live a carefree life?*

*No waiting, no wishing—just being.*


### *Letting Go*

*Sometimes, we just don't want to do or feel anything at all—*

*No schemes, no worries, no love affairs, no attachments.*

*We wish to forget it all, to let our thoughts drift,*

*Flowing with life, with no strings attached.*

*Tomorrow might bring storms or danger,*

*But for now, why not set aside everything?*

*The relationships, the tasks, the plans—*

*Let them all rest until tomorrow.*

*Storms will come and go. There's nothing new under the sun.*

*Relax and wait. Tomorrow may arrive with clear skies,*

*And even the storm in your heart may fade away.*

*Become empty—just let go.*

## 12. NATION AND PEOPLE

The word "nation" carries a certain sacredness. It represents the place of our birth, the land where we are united under one big roof, taught to see each other as brothers and sisters, all from the same roots and ancestors.

In Vietnam, we even call each other "dong bao," meaning we come from the same womb. According to legend, a hundred men hatched from a hundred eggs, and from those men, kings rose up to reclaim the land and build regimes.

That's where the nation began, forming the boundaries of our language, customs, and government. Governments change, but the heart of the nation remains. The people remain.

To survive in a fast-moving world, the nation must recognize its weaknesses and adapt. Governments are just the face of the nation for the time being. With every era comes a new government, and choosing that government falls on the people.

Every nation has its share of heroes and villains, noble acts and moments of shame, dreams of victory, and inevitable sins.

So, don't point fingers at the nation. Ask yourself, what era are we in?

## 13. HUMANS

Humans are unpredictable—full of surprises and contradictions. They can be brilliant one moment and astonishingly foolish the next. At times they are both refined and crass, passionate but also indifferent, brave yet occasionally cowardly. You'll see someone fiercely determined one day, and hopelessly lost the next.

People can be noble, yet sometimes they'll stoop to petty actions; honest one moment, and bending the truth the next—all depending on the situation and the time.

To describe someone's character is to merely scratch the surface, only glimpsing what's visible. Beneath that exterior is a deeper nature, hidden behind a collection of masks that rarely fall.

People are ever-changing, their essence a delightful puzzle. It's the way they continuously evolve that keeps life interesting—an endless parade of mystery, quirks, and charm.

So if you're ever confused by a person's actions, just remember: it's humans who add the color and chaos to life. And isn't that what makes this unpredictable ride so much fun?

## 14. DRIVERS

I've learned a surprising amount from drivers. Their personalities are more varied than you'd expect, each with their own quirks and wisdom, wrapped in a rugged, adaptable charm.

One driver used to work for an Eastern European security agency. He loved reading newspapers. Once, I was in a mad rush and told him to wait with the engine running while I quickly signed some papers. I came back 30 minutes later to find him engrossed in the news. "Where's the car?" I asked. He looked up slowly and, without missing a beat, said, "Another agency driver took it." Well, of course, he did.

Another driver had military experience. He'd be a lieutenant-colonel if he'd stayed in the army, and I often called him by that rank. One day, after a minor accident, we were being chased. He drove straight into a ripening rice field, stopped the car, opened the door, and said, "You're the leader, I'll take the blame. Walk home." There I was, standing in the middle of golden rice under the afternoon sun, with no idea where to go. This man, clearly a strategist of sorts, left me stranded in a sea of rice. But hey, at least he was experienced, right?

Then there was the young driver with the Buddha-like ears. I could scold him all day, and he'd just smile back at me. He was a saint, always making sure I was comfortable, well-fed, and cared for—never letting my outbursts affect him. If Zen had a chauffeur, it would be him.

Another driver once got fed up with my yelling in a traffic jam. I was irritated by the loud music, and he had enough. Right there, in the middle of the congested street, he turned off the engine, stepped out, and left me sitting in the car. I'll never forget that moment. He might have just walked off, but the courage it took to abandon me in traffic? That's a rare kind of bravery.

Then there was the monk-like driver with a crew cut who never spoke much. He prepared everything for me on trips—clothes, medicine, even condoms—without a single complaint. He was calm, silent, and dedicated, no matter how loud or unreasonable I got in the backseat.

These drivers were more than just people behind the wheel—they were my teachers, each one brave, patient, devoted, and unshakeable. Thank you, my friends. You're truly wonderful.

## 15. SECURITY GUARDS

Security guards aren't exactly known for being chatty or overly friendly, but they possess a certain simplicity and an almost admirable endurance. Their day consists of short bursts of activity when cars or people come through—otherwise, they're glued to screens, occasionally scrolling through their phones or tapping away at some game. Maybe they exchange a few words with a colleague or wander off to their little corner of the building, but the chaos of the world outside? Not their problem.

They have a curious calm about them, a sense of peace with their surroundings. They work and live in the same space, completely unfazed by the busyness that comes and goes around them. It's like they've figured something out that the rest of us are too busy to notice. Everything can be moving, changing, or falling apart, but there they are—steady, content, and unbothered. Maybe, just maybe, we could learn something from their stillness.

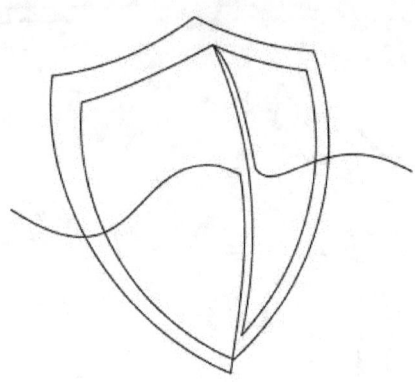

## 16. SENSE OF HUMOR

People often take their life plans way too seriously. Success is elusive, and when things don't go as planned, they stew in anger, wallow in negative thoughts, and occasionally flirt with failure. The dream of conquering the summit of one's career often turns life into a grueling slog.

But there's a secret charm in mediocrity, simplicity, and letting things flow. It's like taking the scenic route instead of speeding on the highway. That said, if you get too comfortable with mediocrity, it can slowly pull you down like a comfy couch you never want to leave.

So here's the trick: live with serious intentions, but embrace the mediocre moments with a grin. Laugh at yourself. Let life throw you a curveball, and if you miss it, laugh even harder.

In the end, humor is the best safety net. It cushions your falls and makes even the most frustrating detours worthwhile.

## 17. DEDICATION

To the Nation's call, I dedicate my genuine zeal.

To my parents' call, I dedicate my loving heart.

To a teacher's call, I dedicate my strong will.

To my lover's needs, I dedicate my excited body.

Dedication is a fancy word attached to noble deeds. It's like this magical feeling that makes us feel heroic and enchanted, like we're part of something grand.

But, be honest—do you have anything truly precious left for dedication?

Our bodies get worn out by fruitless love.

Our will fades after long days of hustling just to pay the bills.

Our hearts flicker from missed chances.

And our zeal? Well, it cools down with broken promises.

So, before you go tossing around your grand ideas of dedication, do yourself a favor and purge. Seriously, clean house. You should be noble if you plan to dedicate yourself to anything noble.

Make your body strong, clean, and built to endure.

Make your mind rich, sharp, and wise.

Make your heart full of love, sweetness, and a willingness to share.

Make your zeal awake, tireless, and ready to ignite again.

Once you've done that, congratulations—you've become something greater. You'll find within yourself the essence of the Nation, your parents, your teachers, your lovers, and your friends. And guess what? You won't have to chase vanity anymore, because now you're the Creator, dedicating yourself to something divine.

## 18. WOMEN

Women love gifts and the search for meaningful connections. They have a unique talent for reinventing themselves, staying attractive not just in appearance but in their ever-evolving sense of self. It's an art form they've mastered.

Thanks to their nurturing instincts, women often display a maturity that surprises even themselves. They sometimes see their partners as a bit like sulky kids who need a gentle hand. Instead of overanalyzing, they rely on a keen intuition, which is often more accurate than a long investigation. Yet, just when you think you've got them all figured out, they add a twist—keeping life interesting with their emotional depth.

Men, on the other hand, often find themselves drawn to physical beauty, while women seek emotional adventures. What makes a woman truly captivating isn't just her looks but her ability to offer a mix of sweetness and challenge. It's the blend of these emotions that makes a relationship worth chasing, even if it sometimes feels like trying to catch lightning in a bottle.

When a woman loves, she does it wholeheartedly. She may take risks that seem bold, or even shocking, driven by passion. While men might grumble through betrayal and eventually let go, women rarely forget. They value loyalty deeply and won't easily forgive when it's broken. Women enjoy the thrill of connection and tend to appreciate confidence—so a little courage goes a long way.

In the end, women are one of life's most intriguing mysteries. Approach them with respect, understanding, and maybe a bit of humor. After all, navigating the complexities of love and life is a journey best taken with a smile.

## 19. MEN

Men often tread lightly on the surface of life, especially when it comes to love. They like to think of themselves as brave heroes, destined for some grand mission, and set out on a journey for "truth." Along the way, though, they tend to get distracted. They're not exactly known for sharing deep thoughts—especially with anyone they don't find reliable. So, in their travels, a lover who offers warmth and a willing ear might mistakenly be elevated to the status of "*soulmate*." And just like that, a man may stumble upon several "*soulmates,*" particularly at the more dangerous curves of life's winding roads.

To a man, every love affair feels like a dazzling adventure. Perhaps it's the rush of excitement, or maybe it's just the exhaustion from the journey, but at some point, he might decide that this particular soulmate is "the one." And so begins the long journey of what was once a short-term insanity. A man's life from that point on is marked by what we call long-term foolishness. And as time goes on, the urge to take on new adventures and new soulmates might resurface. You can guess what happens next—he dives headfirst into another round of idiocy, much to his own surprise.

Then, one day, perhaps on a quiet autumn afternoon, he suddenly wakes up. It dawns on him that maturity is less about heroics and more about understanding what it truly means to be alone. That's when a man finally understands himself— right there in his solitude.

191

## 20. LOVE

Love has no eyes; it follows wherever the blind heart leads.

Love has no logic either; it runs on stirred-up emotions.

It's love that whisks you away to a strange land, filled with both physical joy and ultimate illusions.

It's love that encourages you to do extraordinary—and let's be honest—completely ridiculous things, all while making nonsense seem like perfect sense.

It's love that wraps you in a soft, pleasant-smelling coat, while secretly laying out a bed of nails for you to fall on.

It's love that trains your patience to endure every hardship while, at the same time, turning you into an impudent, sadistic brute when you least expect it.

Love will strip you down to your bare skin but have you believing you're nothing less than an angel.

Love, of course, isn't selfish at all—except for that tiny detail where it's all about possession.

Love doesn't hand you happiness, but oh, the ecstatic satisfaction is real.

Love isn't calm waters; it's a wild ride that shakes you up and leaves you lost.

It demands songs of praise and devotion.

It lights up your sleeping willpower and fuels your courage.

It gives you softness, but also brings pain.

It demands both your cheer and your tears, and teaches you how to be grateful, how to truly appreciate this wild life we're living.

Love is a restive horse, sometimes kicking your rear on the way to the climax.

And yet, love makes you fully human in the truest sense—not noble, not despicable, just human.

It's the source of both our greatest creations and our wildest destructions.

## 21. MUSIC

The quartet is playing passionately, filling the room with vibrant harmonies while the soft drink vendor adds his own, less melodic, accompaniment from the back.

This band hadn't been together for too long, but their leader was a renowned musician who had returned home to reunite with three old friends. As she introduced them, it became obvious that her bandmates were no novices either, having toured many places before.

As they reached the climax of the piece, the women seemed to melt into the music. Their bodies swayed with every note, their arms moved with precision, and their heads tilted back as if lost in a daydream. They were captivating—art in motion.

The audience erupted in applause. The leader, suddenly shy, thanked everyone for their kindness. Her trio played beautifully, each note delivered with sincerity. In the glow of the stage lights, I noticed something amusing: her bust, waist, and hips were almost the same size. It struck me as both peculiar and charming—an artist whose sincerity clearly transcended the physical form.

They were musicians through and through—honest, real, and entirely captivating, even if a bit geometrically balanced.

## 22. REGRET

I sometimes take my uncle to the golf course. Despite being in his eighties, he always shows up looking sharp and cheerful. Whether walking or riding in the golf cart, he handles everything like a pro. He often reminds me to relax. Miss the ball? No big deal—take another shot. If it lands in a bunker or rolls into the bushes, he just says, "We'll dig it out."

His scores are pretty low, but that's because he occasionally swings and misses. Still, he's always content. After the game, we sit down for a meal. He eats with a hearty appetite, laughing and chatting away like we're the same age. He'll tell me, "I get regular check-ups—kidneys, liver, stomach, heart, eyes—all in great shape."

And he's right. He looks great, all things considered. Then, as a pretty waitress walks by, he goes quiet for a moment, watching her with a wistful look. After a pause, he leans in and sighs, "But, you know, that *one* thing doesn't move like it used to."

We both burst out laughing. Some regrets, it seems, come with a sense of humor.

## 23. THE ART OF STILLNESS

### *Incense Offering to the Buddha*

In the quiet of early morning or the calm of late afternoon, I find myself tidying up the worship room. I light a candle, offer incense, pour fresh water into small cups, and gather fallen flower petals. The bell's soft chime reverberates, and I sit in silence. Outside the room, the clamor of daily life and its worries are left behind. In here, I sink into the scent of incense, letting it carry me away. *Quiet.*

*Empty.*

*Endless.*

### *Meditation as a Kind of Living Art*

Meditation brings the mind to stillness, focusing on simplicity, purity, and harmony with nature. It's about clearing out the clutter and excess. When you're fully present in something—whether dining, bathing, gardening, or even enjoying a cup of tea—every moment turns into a work of art. It's about living peacefully, gracefully, and fully in the now.

Those who meditate remove themselves from life's noise and chaos, inching closer to a pure existence. The goal isn't complex. Strip away greed, the excess of modern life, and all the unnecessary distractions. Your environment, too, plays a role in shaping your soul. Imagine a green garden, a mossy stone, and a pebble path. They offer peace, a sense of time, and the quiet joy of simplicity.

People must hustle to make a living, and the world keeps moving fast. But the greatest joy is finding that inner calm, that stillness, even when the world refuses to slow down.

# 24. MARKS OF PERFECTION

## *Perfection*

Perfection is like a shining peak that calls us all—whether it's a flawless work of art, an exceptional plan, or even a perfectly sculpted mind or body. We each have a responsibility to pursue it, to strive for that pinnacle in one area of life, and not necessarily in every aspect. Achieving perfection in any field is a rare and noble feat. It drives us forward, pushing us to train harder, stay creative, and keep evolving.

But here's the catch: perfection isn't static. It shifts with time, place, and circumstance. What was once perfect may not be so tomorrow. The pursuit of perfection leads us to compete, to innovate, and to grow—but it also exhausts us.

The irony? Few people realize that the truest perfection might be within us, quietly waiting to be found.

## *Personal Mark*

We all have our own ways of leaving marks on the world. Some do it with grand gestures—monuments, immortalized works of art, heroic deeds. Others leave their mark with love, pure and endless.

Yet sometimes, the simplest things endure: the banyan tree shading a village square, the melody of a country song, or the refreshing water of an old well. These simple pleasures may not be written in history books, but they live in our hearts, passed down through time.

Today, I saw a newly planted tree at an ancient pagoda, its roots still fresh in the earth. Below it, a copper plate bore a noble name and title, etched for posterity.

I couldn't help but smile. Perhaps the real legacy isn't the name on the plate but the shade that tree will one day provide to weary travelers. Old marks, like ancient people, never truly fade. They simply linger, waiting to meet us again in another life.

## 25. DRUNK

That soft, floaty state that seems to free us from the dull weight of everyday emotions. When we're drunk, everything loosens—our conversations flow, our smiles widen, and we listen to each other as if the world suddenly makes sense.

I met him by chance one autumn afternoon at my friend's art gallery opening. He waved me over, pulling me close like an old confidant. After listening intently to the artist rambling on about his "ultimate feelings," he turned to me and said, "I like this guy."

"Yeah, he seems to live in his own prolonged insanity. Great man material, for sure. You've got a bit of that going on yourself."

"You're calling me insane, aren't you?"

"Right. We're both insane. But you're definitely more insane than I am."

We navigated through the gallery crowd, exchanging greetings and handshakes, surrounded by walls filled with art that oozed physical attraction. Every few minutes, I had to pull him away from groups of his fans who were eager to hear him talk about new painting techniques and technology. He's a true genius, I think.

Eventually, I whisked him away to a quiet pub with hardly any diners. The restaurant owner herself set the table for us, kind and attentive as if we were the only two people in the world. After a few glasses of deep, sweet wine and endless debate about great men and their shared madness, he suddenly turned to me and asked if I wanted to hear the story of the miraculous person who had changed his life.

"Of course," I said. It's a story I've heard him tell at least five times over the years, whenever we meet like this. It's always filled with wise advice from a mysterious figure who apparently had all the answers. The problem is, I always forget the details once I'm drunk again. But I listened, staring at him with rapt attention, hoping this time I'd remember it all.

We drank more white wine and devoured roe together, the sound of old country music filling the air, taking us back to simpler times. I wanted to thank the restaurant owner for her hospitality, but suddenly, he stood up and announced, "I've gotta go. I've got another date."

I walked him to the door, watching him disappear into the empty street as the early autumn wind sent shivers through the night. I knew he was off to meet another VIP.

I returned to our table, feeling no particular urge to be anywhere else. My glass was still full, the restaurant owner's soft words filled the air around me, and her brother called over a leggy waitress to keep me company. The music grew louder, and before I could even consider feeling lonely, a fresh-faced novice appeared with a cigar in hand, ready to join the fun. I was getting tipsy, sinking into that sweet insanity among friends, while the lights outside flickered like the world had momentarily paused just for us.

# 26. WHISPERS AND RUMORS

## *Bragging*

At men's gatherings, after the usual banter about work or a few sips of wine, the topic often shifts to stories about relationships. The conversation can drift from past romances to new loves, and somehow, the tales always seem to grow with every retelling. Each man seems to claim a heroic ability in the art of charm. Oddly enough, failures are rarely mentioned, and the exaggeration of their "conquests" can sound like a fishing story—the fish just gets bigger every time.

It's a bit comical, really. What starts as a lighthearted chat often turns into a contest of sorts, as if they're trying to convince themselves as much as their audience. Yet, by the end of the evening, with their glasses empty, they grow more reflective, even sympathetic. Suddenly, the bravado fades, and they speak with a tenderness, as if they've realized that life, and love, isn't just about grand tales, but the quieter moments in between.

But what about women? Do they share the same kind of stories when they gather? I imagine their conversations might be more thoughtful, possibly deeper, perhaps not so focused on embellishment, but on understanding. I like to think they speak more about their own experiences and emotions, with less need for flair. But who knows? The mysteries of conversation over wine remain.

## *The Public*

The "public" is a curious thing. It's hard to pinpoint exactly who or what it is—sometimes it's a person, sometimes a group, sometimes just a whisper carried on the wind. And yet, the public seems to know everything. They offer opinions on anything, and they do it with confidence, whether or not they truly understand. They're often quick to judge, and that judgment can feel like it's hanging over you, even when you don't know where it came from.

The public can be harsh, even cruel at times, but also strangely indifferent. They have this knack for fueling rumors—clear one day, vague the next. And though their opinions can seem overwhelming, in the end, you have to wonder: who are they really? Perhaps they're just people, like you and me, muddling through life, trying to make sense of it all.

It's easy to feel resentment towards the public, especially when their judgment feels misplaced or unfair. But the truth is, the public's power lies mostly in perception. If you live your life modestly, with a bit of mystery, the public can't grasp you as easily. And maybe that's the trick—to live in a way that's honest to yourself, while keeping just enough distance from the world's opinion to stay grounded.

## 27. ORIGIN

I've wandered across the country on foot, meeting people who might share the same last name but whose voices are as different as the landscapes they come from.

In the Northwest, their voices dart around like they're in a hurry, light and fast, as if they're singing a song that occasionally remembers to be in our language. Midnorth folks, on the other hand, speak with a softness that feels like slipping into a cozy, familiar old sweater—it just fits. Then there are the coastal dwellers, whose speech crashes through the air with a rhythm as forceful as the ocean tides. And don't get me started on the rice-growing regions of the Northern Delta. Their voices carry the scent of fresh earth and bamboo, with an endearing twist. They swap their "n"s and "l"s so casually, making "eat," "beautiful," "butterfly," and "flower" sound like the sweetest mix-up you've ever heard.

Now, the folks from the Central Region? Well, their accents are an entirely different ballgame. You need to be on your A-game just to follow the conversation, but the moment they start singing? Oh, boy. That gruffness melts into a song that stays with you like the chorus of your favorite tune stuck in your head.

Down South, their voices have this gentle, homesick vibe, like they've been away for a while but haven't quite let go. And let me tell you, the wine talks here? Absolute gold. No rules—just free-flowing words, laughter, and the occasional outrageous story that may or may not be true.

Capital people speak with a kind of elegant restraint, as if they're always minding their manners. Meanwhile, the people of Central North are full of energy and charm, as if they're always ready to welcome you with open arms and a few funny stories.

And then there are the girls across the country. Their voices and emotions are like a country song—some are sweet, some are sassy, but all have a story behind them. There's a lifetime hidden in a single word, one little laugh, or even in a whispered secret that could mean anything depending on the accent.

## 28. HATRED

Those who've been in love know what real hatred feels like. It's that fiery emotion that somehow fills the gap left by love's demise, though ironically, it's a bit of a flaw in the design.

We're often told hatred is a weakness, the coward's way out. But let's be honest—hatred sometimes disguises itself as pride. That same stubborn pride that stops you from texting your ex at 2 a.m.

When a nation is swept up in hatred, oddly enough, it can become the fuel for patriotism. Suddenly, everyone's ready to fight a war—whether it's against an actual enemy or just against whoever left the milk out of the fridge again.

But here's the catch: hatred never truly goes away as long as love exists. It's like a flame that flickers out only to reignite when you least expect it—just when you thought you'd moved on, there it is, smoldering again.

When people feel hatred, they're usually too wrapped up in their own emotions to think straight. But, if they focus their energy in the right direction, well, they can turn into a force of nature—though, let's hope it's for the good.

So, hatred isn't exactly cowardice. In fact, it's more like the misguided sibling of courage, with love being its complicated, overdramatic mother.

But love—oh love!—it's tangled up with desire, attachment, and yes, a bit of lust. As the Buddha wisely told us, the goal is to live with compassion, free from greed, hatred, and ignorance.

Easier said than done, though. Honestly, I'm still trying to figure it all out.

## 29. CHILDHOOD PERFORMANCE

Most things in life slip away with time, but there are a few glorious—and, yes, mortifying—moments that stick to your memory like glue.

I had one of those moments. It all came flooding back when I happened to pass by the old school I attended.

It was the end of the school year, and my best friend and I decided to register for the closing ceremony talent show. We were going to perform "Hey Jude" by The Beatles. My friend was going to sing, and I'd accompany him on guitar. We even came up with this overly dramatic introduction, hoping to give everyone something memorable to talk about before the summer break.

We went through a few qualifying rounds in cramped classrooms, and, suddenly, we were *the* guys. The future rock stars of the school. People whispered and pointed as we walked around the schoolyard during breaks. Our heads were so big, I'm surprised we could still get through the doors.

Finally, the big day arrived. The Youth Union kicked things off with some humorous skits, and then it was our turn. We were full of excitement as we took the stage. The whole school fell into this intense silence. My friend gave his heartfelt intro, then launched into the vocals. I strummed along with my guitar, feeling like we were *nailing* it.

But...something felt off. It turns out, the microphone was broken. So while my friend belted his heart out, no one heard a single note. The only thing the audience got was an awkward solo from me and my guitar.

When we finished, one of our classmates ran up to the stage and said, "Hey, this microphone's dead. We only heard the guitar."

Oh. My. Gosh. We had no clue and just went on, blissfully performing for an audience that wasn't hearing a word of it. The embarrassment was real.

For the next two weeks, we avoided everyone. We'd show up early and leave late, like we were on some kind of self-imposed witness protection program. We didn't dare make eye contact with anyone—two fallen stars trying to survive the humiliation.

204

If only we could've done it again! Ah, childhood...

## 30. SWEETHEARTS

You've been with me for years, holding so many of my memories. I got to know you when I was still a kid, sometimes in public, sometimes in secret. I remember hustling, selling newspapers just to have enough money for you. Sometimes, you'd follow me home after a chance encounter at the library. Other times, I had to fight off my friends to keep you. When I left my hometown, you came with me, never leaving my side. You'd whisper to me, offer advice, get a little moody, and sometimes even weep quietly. You stirred up emotions in me that I never expected.

I've brought you back from faraway places, and you've seen me at my worst, during my hardest days. I spent my modest scholarship and meager earnings on you, happily. When I lived alone in that noisy city, I'd visit you by the lake full of willows. You'd comfort me while everyone else was heading home or while the homeless men nearby sat in their own worlds. You've been with me through vibrant summers, bittersweet autumns, frigid winters, and blooming springs of love. You've been my lover and my closest companion—loyal, steadfast, never betraying me. You hold onto my good old days like a treasure chest of memories.

But then, yesterday, it hit me like a ton of bricks. I'd been so caught up chasing after the constant demands of life that I forgot all about you. I left you tucked away in a corner, neglected. And what did the termites do? They had a feast. My sweethearts... you're not what you used to be.

You are my old books. The ones that still stand humbly next to the bright, flashy new ones on my shelf. Only now, you're hollowed out. Just faded covers and crumbling pages.

I couldn't help but feel a pang of sadness, holding your worn and torn pages in my hands. How quickly life moves on.

## 31. SEEING A DOCTOR MEANS COMFORT

I had a general check-up today. Been feeling tired lately—sometimes dizzy too. The cold wind's rolling in, hinting that another season's on its way.

So, I went through all the tests, handed over the results, and the doctor started scribbling some hieroglyphs on his notepad. He looked up and said:

"Normal blood pressure. Heart beats a little slow. Liver and kidneys are doing their thing. Blood sugar—normal. Leukocytes, intestines—good. Triglycerides? A bit high. Uric acid? On the higher side too. Cholesterol? Also a bit up there. But overall, these numbers are pretty standard for someone in their forties."

"Wait," I interrupted. "I had a check-up last year. Same 'normal' speech, but these levels weren't this high."

Earlier this year, my wife dragged me to a Chinese medicine practitioner. The guy grabbed my wrist, squinted at me, and said to my wife, "His kidneys are weak, especially the yin ones."

I shot her a look that screamed, "You hearing this?" But she just gave me a look that said, "I knew it."

Long story short, I spent the next month drinking some bizarre concoction that tasted like a mix of wet socks and dirt. Didn't feel any different, though. Couldn't even bring myself to finish the bottle.

"Doc," I said, lowering my voice. "I'm feeling kinda... weak, you know? Like, the flame's just not there at home. Could it be my 'yin kidneys'? The Chinese medicine guy told me they're shot."

The doc chuckled. "Nah, your kidneys are fine. Your heart's just beating a bit slow, which means you've got mild anemia. Sometimes, that messes with your head and your... you know, 'enthusiasm.' There's no yin or yang kidneys, trust me."

I nodded, feeling relieved but a little deflated. "You ever feel like that?"

He grinned. "Of course! Everybody's been there. Don't stress."

So, I waved goodbye, went home, and tossed the medicine in the cabinet—right next to last year's forgotten stash. I figured, I'd take two-thirds of the pills, go vegetarian for a few days, and then get back to my usual wine and steak routine.

Because really, seeing the doctor? It's just for comfort.

## 32. NEVER SEE OLD MEMORIES AGAIN

When I went abroad for school, I took with me a little photo album of my family, friends, and a few special people. The photos were black and white, but in my mind, they were as colorful as ever. Whenever homesickness hit hard, I'd flip through those pages and revisit the past.

On the very first page, I placed a photo of my girlfriend—big smile, long hair, bright eyes, and those unforgettable dimpled cheeks. The photo might have been small, but the memory? Oh, it was larger than life. That was my student love, full of emotions, dreams, and everything in between.

There were graduation day snapshots too. I promised myself that as soon as I returned home, I'd revisit our old school and, of course, reunite with my old flame. But life got busy. After ten years abroad, I came back and work swallowed me whole. It took two more years before I had a chance to visit the past.

When I finally made it back, the schoolyard—once shaded by that old tree, with its moss-covered octagonal pavilion, flower-lined paths meandering by West Lake—was no more. Instead, I found roads under construction, newly built houses, and the lake embanked. Nostalgia hit hard, and I couldn't shake the sadness for an entire month.

As for my student love, she'd vanished. I had no idea where she went. Then one scorching day, as I sped down a familiar street, someone called my name. I stopped, looked around, and saw nothing but dracontomelon trees, their flowers releasing that sweet, familiar scent. In the distance, I noticed a freight bicycle with big baskets full of bananas and two figures standing beside it. One was busy with the bananas, while the other waved at me.

Curious, I walked closer. The one waving was pregnant and holding a bunch of bananas in her other hand. My heart skipped a beat.

Wait, could this be...?

I looked again. My heart sank. It was her—my student love, now just casually buying bananas on the side of the road, her life so different from what I'd imagined.

At that moment, I realized something: some memories are best left untouched. Now I know why.

## 33. SOLITARY AS A REMINDER

Last weekend, I convinced a friend to escape to the suburbs with me for a peaceful stroll around a lake. We figured we'd turn over some soil, toss some grass around like we knew what we were doing, and simply enjoy the beauty of the rustic countryside. You know, the kind of day that makes you feel like a character in an old novel.

We stopped at a roadside food stall for lunch. After placing our order, we wandered off to kill time. When we returned, the food was already waiting for us, like a well-timed surprise—crunchy vegetables, delicious sesame, savory meat, and, of course, good wine. Life was suddenly as easy as it could get.

Out of nowhere, I heard loud chatter coming from the next table. Two men were sitting there, one eagerly picking at his food with chopsticks, the other pouring wine like he was on a mission. They looked like they were having the time of their lives—autumn had that effect. The air was crisp, a few leaves had fallen in front of the porch, and in the distance, we could hear a rooster crowing from some hidden garden. It felt like a scene from another time.

As the wine flowed, so did the conversation. I couldn't help but think: a thousand years ago, men probably sat just like this, talking loudly over wine at some empty roadside stall in autumn. Nothing's really changed, I thought. The same excitement, the same simple joys.

Then, it started raining. The road outside became slick and empty, save for a single truck that roared past, disturbing the calm for just a moment before it too disappeared. A steaming dish of chicken was brought to our table. More wine, more murmured conversations as the rain fell outside.

For a brief moment, I pictured a horse-drawn carriage passing by instead of the truck, splashing through the same autumn rain on the same old path. And I thought, yes, some things never change. Time moves forward, but some moments stay the same—small, timeless reminders of how solitary and connected we all are.

## 34. HAIRCUT DAY

Life's full of good days and bad days, auspicious and not-so-auspicious days. Nobody can really explain why certain days get the lucky stamp, but somehow, they do. It's like a cosmic shrug. "Today's good, tomorrow's iffy." You just go with it.

People are funny that way. We love breaking taboos but still secretly want to cover our bases, like we're hoping karma is taking notes. Maybe the universe—or some kindly deity—takes pity on us and throws us a few signals. Thus, the idea of 'lucky days' was born.

For the most part, we live by three different calendars. The Western one keeps us on track for work and social obligations. The Lunar calendar? That's for the traditions—honoring our ancestors, celebrating the moon festivals. And then there's this mystical, cosmic calendar for the days we hope to get right with the universe, purify our souls, and maybe, just maybe, win some divine favor.

Take me, for instance. On the first and 15th of the lunar month, I'm all about incense offerings to Buddha and my ancestors, and I keep a vegetarian diet for good measure. I steer clear of big life decisions, or anything that requires energy (yup, even that) during the San Niang Killing Days—those 5th, 14th, and 23rd days when the universe is apparently in a mood.

And haircuts? Well, I save those for the last day of the month, when I can indulge in a ritualistic slow-motion shave, splash some water on my body, and savor the whole experience. It's not just grooming; it's a cosmic reset.

I'm convinced the universe smiles on a well-timed haircut.

## 35. LIAR

I've never been a fan of liars. They all have a few telltale signs: they can't seem to look you in the eye—though they might glance sideways as if checking to see if their story is holding up. They speak quickly, stumble through excuses, and love to dance around the point. With imaginations as thin as paper, they sprinkle in details that sound just real enough.

After a while, they get so used to lying, they start believing their own nonsense. It's a bit like a magic trick gone wrong—except the only one who's fooled is the magician. The more they lie, the more they rely on their own fabrications to navigate life. It's like they're building a house of cards on a windy day and somehow convinced it's hurricane-proof.

What's even more fascinating is how they draw on scraps of reality. They take a kernel of truth, season it with their imagination, and serve up a tall tale, garnished with just the right amount of threats or gossip to keep it interesting. And if you catch them in their lies? They're quick with excuses, slipping into a syrupy tone when talking about love or gratitude. They know how to put on a good act, all while hiding their cowardice behind a mask of hard work and self-sacrifice.

The problem with liars is that their dishonesty spreads like a virus. One coward infects the next, and soon the whole place is full of people copying each other's lies. It's contagious, and the only cure is to call it out before it takes over.

But for the liars themselves? Telling lies becomes a disease, something that sticks with them. It's worse than betrayal because, unlike a one-time backstab, lying becomes their way of life. An incurable condition that only gets worse with age.

## 36. JAIL

No matter what we're doing—working hard for a living, wandering through unfamiliar places, or simply staring out of the window of a quiet room—sooner or later, we come to a startling realization: we're all living the life of prisoners. And here's the kicker—it's not the world that built our cells, it's us. We've managed to construct these cozy yet monotonous jails ourselves. A lovely, boring prison—complete with our favorite habits, comforts, and rituals.

It feels like this was always meant to be, doesn't it? Alongside us in this strange incarceration are our fellow inmates—accomplices in the crime of routine. Alone, or sometimes in eager company, we march side by side, shackled by the chains of habit, dogma, and the endless rituals we pretend are necessary.

When did this happen? When did we voluntarily throw ourselves into this prison of comfort and predictability? And more importantly, why does it no longer feel stifling but almost... familiar? Why did the fire in our hearts cool down, leaving us to simply accept everything, day after day?

There's a sense that no matter where we go or what we try, we're under constant surveillance—thousands of invisible eyes watching our every move, thought, and word. It's almost laughable how often we think we're breaking free, only to find ourselves right back in the same cell, as if our escape routes were really just well-disguised loops.

So, we stay here—day in, day out, sentenced to life in our own self-made cages. But now, we finally understand why they say death is the ultimate freedom. After all, it's the only way out of the jail we've been building brick by brick.

And oddly enough? That realization is kind of... pleasant.

# 37. THE SWING OF LIFE

## *The Swing*

Before each swing, he makes a series of solemn moves, almost like a sacred ritual. He bends his knees slightly, bows his head, and grips the club in front of the ball with the seriousness of a knight preparing for battle. He stares at the ball as if it holds the meaning of life, then lifts his head, taking in the vast horizon as if seeking wisdom from the golf gods above. Then, with the utmost grace, he bends down again, turns his body just so, lifts his arms, and then—*whack*—the club slices through the air.

His body twists in perfect harmony with the swing, his right leg turning until he's on his toes, hands elegantly sweeping over his shoulder, head locked in place like a statue. Only after a few reverent seconds does he allow himself to watch the ball sail through the air, usually with a hint of regret, as if it didn't quite live up to the majestic form of the swing. But oh, what a perfect move it was, like a dance choreographed to precision.

Every weekend, without fail, he heads to the golf course, dressed not in the stern, simple attire of his weekday work but in colorful clothes and bold shoes that scream *celebration.* It's like a mini festival for him, a retreat from the drudgery of work. The course is his sanctuary, his stage, and he plays his part with reverence.

## *Complaint*

Yet, despite his weekend transformation, when we walk together through the field, sit in the same car, or share a table at a party, the facade falls. He often opens up, his calm demeanor cracking just enough for the complaints to trickle out—about work, the endless difficulties with officials, the ever-changing policies that seem as stable as a house of cards.

He's a man of few words, usually reserved and careful, even in the heat of a game. He doesn't get ruffled by jokes or silly banter like others do. If he joins in, it's only with the most delicate of comments, like a fine wine that refuses to be gulped.

But once we're alone, he pours out his frustrations with the same care he puts into his golf swing. And I can't help but nod in agreement—so much of what he says feels true. He's spent his career navigating the absurdities of bureaucracy, waiting patiently for retirement, much like he waits for that perfect swing.

And as he swings, it's as if he's not just hitting the ball—he's swiping at the endless annoyances of life, knowing full well that no matter how perfect the form, there's always a bit of regret in the distance.

## 38. LOST IN THE ECHOES

### *Wandering*

Some days, you find yourself adrift. Not lost, exactly, just…floating. You don't know what to do, and the thought of doing anything feels like an unreasonable demand. So, you walk. Aimlessly.

You stroll along the streets, watching people dart by with purpose, as if you've slipped into some other dimension where you're just a bystander. The world hums with activity—people rushing, hustling under rows of trees—but to you, it's all on mute. Your legs move without any particular plan, guiding you through intersections, turning points, and street corners, but your mind? Your mind is somewhere else entirely.

You catch yourself feeling like an outsider, half-witted and dreamlike, wandering through a version of reality that feels just a little off. "Is this a dream?" you ask yourself, and maybe it is. Life feels like a series of intertwined dreams and realities, all blending together until you're no longer sure which one you're in. Perhaps, on days like these, your spirit is taking its own walkabout, occasionally losing its way.

### *Sigh at Night*

Then, there are the nights. You wake up for no reason at all—midnight, the witching hour—and your mind starts its midnight gymnastics. Everything you haven't thought about in a while comes rushing in. You think back to old mistakes, awkward moments, and the things you wish you could redo. And just like that, you sigh. A deep, regretful sigh that echoes in the quiet of the night like a ghost finally letting itself be heard.

You step out onto the balcony, hoping the cool air might shake off the heaviness. The wind stirs the trees, their leaves whispering secrets you can't quite catch. Off in the distance, you hear the soft lap of water against the shore, the occasional splash of a fish breaking the surface before disappearing into the dark.

It's as if everything around you—nature, time, even your memories—has slipped into a deep sleep, leaving only your sigh, lingering in the air, like a soft, regretful exhale from the past. Maybe life really is just a collection of sighs and wanderings. Some days you roam aimlessly through the daylight, other nights you're chasing ghosts in the dark.

## 39. DECENT FIGURE

At 37, she had the kind of beauty that turned heads. An oval face with sparkling eyes that always seemed to be smiling, a nose that looked like it belonged on a Grecian statue, and a dimple that appeared like a secret wink. On crisp autumn days, she'd wear those low-cut shirts that barely hid her curves. Her shoulders were smooth, her hair long and silky, usually swept over one side just enough to reveal a hint of cleavage beneath her snug top. She was fit and carried herself like someone who knew exactly how good she looked.

She was beautiful, graceful, and… a bit complicated.

You see, she was dating two men. At the same time. But this wasn't some reckless fling—no, she was all in. Enthusiastic, passionate, and territorial as a lioness. She managed to keep her two loves neatly divided, confident that no one knew her little secret. She shooed away other women like they were flies buzzing around her territory.

But as secrets tend to go, hers eventually slipped out. One fateful day, the two men bumped into each other, and, to their astonishment, realized they were sharing the same woman.

In her mind, *they* had betrayed *her*—how dare they discover her secret? She retreated behind locked doors, cutting off all contact, nursing her wounds in solitude. The audacity!

Years later, one of those men happened to run into her again on the street. She spotted him and, without a word, turned her back and walked off, still with that same graceful, familiar stride.

He sighed, sipping his coffee beside me. "She's still mad," he said, shaking his head.

Some things never change.

## 40. GOING TO THE RESTROOM

A Buddhist monk once told me that we should focus on everything we do—whether it's eating, walking, sitting, or even something as mundane as going to the restroom. By giving full attention to the task at hand, we achieve mindfulness, and with mindfulness comes calm.

I try to love mindfully, but it's easier said than done. More often than not, while working on one project, I find my mind wandering to the next. It's like flushing the toilet before you've, well… finished. Rushing through life rarely leads to peace.

So, I've turned the restroom into my personal meditation chamber, a place where I can practice focusing. It's small, clean, quiet, and completely private—a perfect sanctuary for mindfulness training.

After I've completed my "business," I linger a little longer with a book in hand. The silence in that tiny room amplifies the sound of turning pages, making it feel as though the outside world has disappeared. In that moment, I'm free, relaxed, and completely present.

Whoever named it the *restroom* really nailed it.

## 41. EXILE AND THE SCENT OF HOME

This afternoon, I'm flying off to a coastal city. Tomorrow morning, a new trip begins. For now, though, I find myself wandering aimlessly down unfamiliar streets. It's autumn, and the leaves are doing their usual dance, swirling around in the air before they finally give up and flop onto the pavement. The street lamps blink on, casting their yellow glow over tightly shut houses, where conversations hum behind closed doors. Pedestrians rush by, all seemingly on a mission to get somewhere important.

And just like that, I'm pulled back to my student days abroad. I used to walk home from school, weaving through streets that felt oddly empty except for the occasional car zipping by. Sometimes, a train would slowly gain speed, its wheels clanging in the distance, leaving behind the kind of hollow echo that makes you feel like the world's holding its breath. The streets rolled on like small hills, quiet and aged, with their dark shadows and their lonely, flickering lights.

Occasionally, I'd catch a glimpse of life behind curtains—people gathered around a table, a woman pouring tea as if the rest of the world didn't exist. There was always laughter, distant and comforting, and every now and then, a window would open, and you'd feel, for a fleeting moment, like you were part of that world. It never failed to make me homesick.

These days, though, home feels more like a series of aisles at the supermarket. Shelves stacked high with everything you need—pre-packaged, pre-sliced, and pre-arranged for maximum convenience. There's no need to pluck chickens or slice meat anymore, not when you've got a fridge full of ready-to-eat meals. It's easy. It's comfortable. It's also incredibly boring. My appetite has become as frozen as the food I pull from the freezer.

But then, one day, you escape the city. You find yourself at a little roadside restaurant on the outskirts of nowhere, and suddenly, you remember what real food tastes like. You wait for your meal, watching the chickens roam freely, clucking away without a care. And when that dish finally arrives—hot, fresh, and full of flavor—it's like a revelation. The chicken's crisp, seasoned with pepper, salt, and lime leaves, and each bite takes you back to a time when food was more than just fuel. It was an experience.

216

The more you travel, the more you realize there's a world beyond supermarket shelves—hill goats, wild boars, rice field crabs, and milk so fresh you can taste the fields it came from. Every dish seasoned with earth, wind, and time, reminding you of what we've lost in our rush for convenience. But, as always, home calls. You pack up and head back to the city, back to the pre-arranged life that's waiting for you.

Still, every now and then, you can't help but think about that roadside restaurant, that fleeting scent of home that lingers in your memory. You can't stay on the road forever, but for a moment, you lived—truly lived—and tasted the world as it was meant to be.

## 42. HOME GARDEN (I)

She'd been busy since we moved into our new house. She kept slipping in and out of the little garden out front, wearing that focused, pensive look she gets when she's hatching a plan. And every day, a new surprise popped up: one day it was some jars and vases, the next it was a few flowerpots, and before I knew it, small bamboo plants had appeared, along with a pomelo tree, and even a jackfruit tree with some impressive jackfruits already hanging beneath the leaves like they'd just materialized there.

Workers came and went, lugging everything from hefty boulders to little pebbles, and after a few weeks away on a business trip, I came home to an incredible sight. Our once-empty garden was now shaded by lush trees, a soft green velvet lawn stretched out like an emerald carpet, and a small pond bubbled peacefully, with purple water lilies standing tall and goldfish darting about like tiny golden arrows. Small bamboo leaves floated lazily on the water, reflecting the sky and clouds above. A quaint stone path wound its way around the garden, as if inviting me for a stroll.

Just as I was taking it all in, a cute little dog burst out of nowhere, barking like he was announcing my arrival to the entire neighborhood. He ran up to me, stood on his hind legs, and waved his front paws like he was trying to give me a formal greeting. His mouth was...well, a bit too enthusiastic. But wow, I had to admit, she'd managed to recreate a charming little corner of a village right in our garden. She was glowing with pride.

But today, when I got home, it was eerily quiet. No sign of the little dog doing his usual circus act to welcome me. She looked glum.

*"Is something wrong, honey?"* I asked, concerned.

*"I locked him up,"* she sighed. *"He dug up half the new lawn in the garden. Absolutely destroyed it. Terrible!"*

Sometimes, even the best-laid plans get a little...dug up.

## 43. HOME GARDEN (II)

Life is full of hustle and worry, a constant race against time. But home, home is where we can kick off our shoes, leave the daily dust and chaos behind, and breathe. And let me tell you, if you can bring even a pinch of nature into your own backyard, it transforms everything. That little garden can become your sanctuary, a place to recharge, unwind, and maybe even reflect on life with a little more calm than you had when you walked in.

Your garden doesn't have to be a botanical masterpiece. It's not about being fancy or shelling out a fortune on exotic plants. No, no—it's about care, simplicity, and a little bit of harmony. Pebbles, green grass, a little moss creeping up the walls—these small touches are where the magic happens. A few carefully pruned shrubs become lush green hills, and a pebble-strewn path invites you to stroll at your leisure. Add in some flowers or grasses that shift with the seasons, and suddenly you've brought the cycle of life right to your doorstep.

Picture this: autumn fades, winter steps in, and the sky and clouds reflect in a small lake, where purple water lilies rise gracefully. Spring wakes up with a rugged peach tree blossoming in pink, while summer brings the sweet scent of pomelo flowers wafting through the house. Bees buzz around like tiny, tireless musicians in a never-ending concert, and the sound of flowing water creates a melody that plays softly in the background—a song of the four seasons, right in your own backyard.

Wander through that garden, let the sounds and scents of the earth wash over you. Find a big rock, sit down, and just breathe. Don't think, don't plan—just let nature seep into your mind, your soul, until everything blooms with quiet serenity. Slowly, the worries of the world fade into the background, like a distant hum. For a while, you become a hermit in your own home, far away from the noise and nonsense that lies outside your door.

Isn't that what we all need? A little peace in a world that keeps pulling us in every direction.

## 44. PROVOCATION

T. is a thirty-year-old mom, gracefully navigating life with a baby on one hip and a curve to her stride that turns heads. She's like a tree in full bloom, vibrant and captivating—everything about her is full, ripe, and just... well, plump. Picture her strutting in heels that seem taller than a skyscraper, her hips swaying like they have a mind of their own. She never walks into a room quietly. No, she *appears*—like magic—from the elevator, from the bathroom, suddenly right there, facing male visitors in the office. Everything about her arrival is perfectly timed, and then—just like that—she's gone, leaving behind a whiff of mystery.

Somehow, these visitors always manage to get her number. And every afternoon, as the office winds down, T. is deep in her phone, busy arranging meet-ups, smiling absentmindedly as she watches traffic go by below.

Today, she arrived at work looking particularly chipper, as though she had shed some heavy weight from her soul. Her friend leaned over and asked, *"What's got you so cheery?"*

With a laugh, T. replied, *"I decided I'm done with dating. Taking a whole month off!"*

*"Really? Why?"*

*"Girl, I've been teetering on tiptoe every night, and then when I get home, I have to rub my own feet and hips back to life..."* she said, exasperated but amused by the absurdity of it all.

I glanced over at her, and something seemed off. She looked... smaller than usual, kind of dainty and sweet. Then I noticed: today, instead of her skyscraper heels, she was wearing simple sandal straps. I couldn't help but smile. Sometimes, a little comfort is the best luxury.

## 45. SPORT

Picture this: young adults chasing each other around a massive green lawn, bumping shoulders, jostling chests, pushing, pulling, and lunging—all in a frenzied effort to capture a tiny ball. When you really think about it, it's kind of absurd. And then there's the crowd—half of them painted in wild green and red face paint, jumping up and down, screaming their lungs out, stomping their feet like toddlers in a tantrum. Drums are pounding, whistles are blowing—it's pure madness.

I suppose this chaotic spectacle has been around for ages—dating back to ancient Roman times or maybe even earlier. The masses have always found some thrill in watching people (or animals!) compete against each other, egged on by the crowd's primal cheers. It's barbaric when you think about it.

Yet, looking back, I must admit, I was once part of that madness myself, back when I was young and full of energy. Back then, I was just like them—caught up in the thrill of the game, not as "refined" as I like to think I am now.

These days, I'm not much for noise or chaos. Give me a quiet, leisurely trip over a rowdy stadium any day. I'm more content wandering familiar paths than competing with anyone. In some ways, I think I'm a bit like a cow—after a long day of work, I just want to wander peacefully through the fields, watch the sun set, and maybe wag my tail a bit. If I'm feeling particularly excited, you might hear a soft "moo" from me, but nothing more. I'm not like the horse that races nonstop, always looking ahead, vying for attention, chest puffed out, hooves clattering with restless energy. No, I'm happy just grazing in the fields, taking life at my own pace.

## 46. IDEAL OF LIFE

Life often feels like a game of resting on our laurels. When we're young, we hustle, trying to travel far and wide, chasing dreams, and competing like it's the Olympics—throw in a little love and sulking, too. Middle age rolls around, and suddenly, we slow down, work moderately, but calculate like pros. We indulge in fancy dinners, chat about national issues as if we're politicians, and judge life like seasoned critics. Then, as we age further, life becomes a slow burn. We count days and months, befriend old trees, and spend time admiring rocks that once seemed, well, just like rocks. We still dream of grand adventures, vast mountains, and uncharted forests, but since no one really listens to us anymore, we stick to giving our offspring life lessons they never asked for.

The truth is, in life, doing something truly monumental is rare. Most of the time, we dabble in small things—things that seem polished and sophisticated at first but turn out to be shallow and soon forgotten. When we can't be strong and imposing, it's best to fake being gentle and elegant. And when we can't be braggadocious, we show restraint and cleverness, even if it leaves us feeling a little weak. Let it be.

A moderate ideal of life wraps everything up in a cozy embrace. It eases the extremes, even softens the more laughable aspects of political theories. It's what makes strict religions like Buddhism feel a bit more approachable for the average person. After all, Buddhism teaches that life is a sea of suffering; everything is impermanent, like a passing cloud or a drop of water. But here's the kicker—if we all suddenly left our worldly lives behind, shaved our heads, and sought refuge under the Buddha's roof, who's taking care of our families? What about our nation? If everyone became monks, who's supporting the monks? Where's the food coming from when there's no one left to beg from?

So, maybe the answer isn't dropping everything and becoming a monk. Maybe it's about being a "monk" right where you are—taking what Buddha taught and applying it at home, in your life.

## 47. A GOOD LAYPERSON

It's tough to be a monk. Staying isolated on a mountain or locked up in a pagoda might sound peaceful, but let's face it—no meat, no wine, no music? That's not just a spiritual cleanse; it's like stripping away all the fun parts of life. Who wouldn't be bored out of their mind?

But here's the thing: even if we indulge in life's pleasures, we often find that joy is fleeting while sorrow lingers. When we're young, we bounce back from heartbreaks and disappointments with ease. But as we get older, those sorrows have a way of sticking around, like uninvited guests who won't leave the party. That's when Buddhist teachings start making sense. If you can't be a full-time monk, why not go part-time? You can stay close to the Buddha's teachings, without giving up the essentials—like family, relationships, and the occasional steak. Just dial down the sensual indulgence a bit.

Speaking of indulgence, let's talk about meat. Sure, it's tasty, but let's not ignore the fact that slaughtering animals is a pretty cruel business. I mean, most of these creatures are downright adorable. Picture this: chopping up an innocent lamb, or mincing some poor little chicken. Heartless, right? But on the other hand, have you tasted lamb chops? Delicious. So, what's a layperson to do? Simple: let someone else do the dirty work. Head to the market, hand off the responsibility to the butcher, and enjoy your meal guilt-free. Men should stay out of the kitchen anyway—that's where all the trouble starts!

Of course, if you listen to your doctor, they'll tell you to ease up on the meat as you get older. Too much red meat? Say hello to high blood pressure. Too much seafood? Watch those joints stiffen up. So maybe the Buddha was onto something with the whole vegetarian thing. Start with a veggie meal or two, just to test the waters. And if you miss meat too much, there are plenty of vegan dishes that taste like meat—sort of. It's good for your health and aligns with the Buddha's teachings, so you're basically scoring bonus karma points with every bite.

But here's the kicker: after a few too many vegetarian meals, you might start feeling a bit...well, off. Your legs feel like jelly, your vision's a little blurry, and let's just say your youthful glow isn't what it used to be. So, maybe don't go full-on vegan just yet. Try a short-term vegan diet—a few days a month or a couple of times a year. Think of it as a spiritual reset. During these days, you should rest,

223

avoid lustful thoughts, and preserve your energy. As you age and your desires naturally fade, that's when you lean more into the monk-like lifestyle. Buddha's all about killing lust, after all.

And hey, if you're balancing all this—some meat, some veggies, a little less lust, and a lot more mindfulness—you've already become a good layperson.

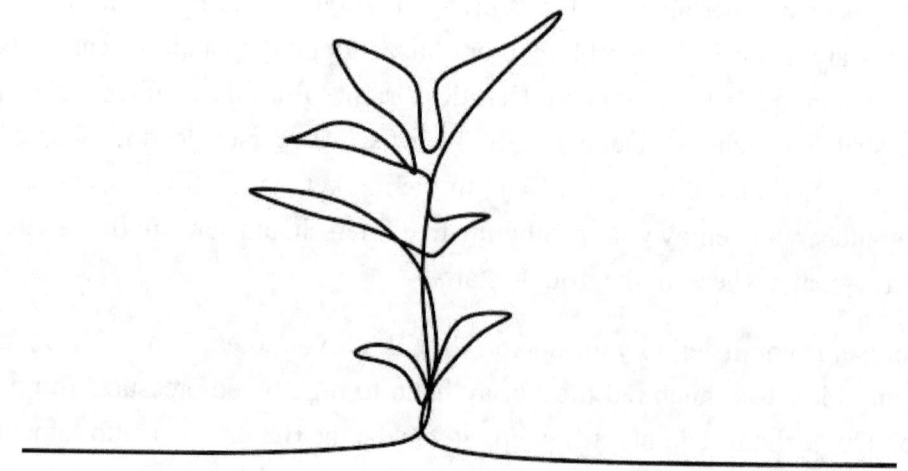

## 48. OUR RELIGIONS

It's no secret that women enjoy visiting pagodas more than men do. Maybe there's something about being in the presence of the Buddha that feels like a warm hug of compassion. Middle-aged women, in particular, flock to these serene spots, chanting with such sincerity you'd think they were serenading the Buddha himself. On holidays and full-moon days, women take their preparations seriously. They head out shopping, carefully select offerings, and—if they can—they'll definitely make a stop at the nearest pagoda. It's a chance to pray, walk among the flowers, and catch up with friends who share the same spiritual inclinations.

Buddhism is like a spiritual gathering place for everyone, opening the Dharma's wide road to men and women alike, inviting them to connect, reflect, and, occasionally, to swap recipes for flower arrangements. Every spring, groups of pilgrims set off for the mountains, navigating bumpy roads and wading through winding rivers, all in the name of reaching some nearly forgotten temple perched on a mountain peak. There, among the clouds, rivers, and sky, they sit and chat about life, mountains, joy, sadness—the whole shebang. After all that, they'll either enjoy a simple vegan meal at the pagoda or feast on rice, wine, and meat at some tiny restaurant by the edge of the forest. It's the ultimate way to let go of the past year's stress and gear up for the one ahead.

And then, of course, there's our other special religion: the Mother Goddess tradition. This one often sneaks in next to the Buddha, just down the road from the pagoda. Temples or palaces dedicated to the Spirits hold ceremonies year-round, celebrating each of the four seasons. At the beginning of the year, people show up to ask for blessings, by mid-year they're sharing their highs and lows while seeking the Spirits' protection, and at year's end, they prepare offerings to express their gratitude.

The star of the ceremony is the medium—not quite male or female but something in between—surrounded by a supportive cast of fellow mediums and followers, all harmonizing to create the perfect spiritual spectacle. The atmosphere starts off reverent and solemn, but before you know it, it's turned into a full-blown festival, complete with velvety musical ensembles and plenty of joy. By the end, everyone's a bit more thoughtful, a bit more compassionate, and somehow closer, like they're all part of one big family under the protective wing of the Mother Goddess.

## 49. WHAT WOMEN WANT

The desire for motherhood is a powerful instinct that nudges young women to enhance their appearance, making them more attractive and confident. They often save from their modest incomes to invest in beauty products, though somehow, it never feels like enough. In the back of their minds, they secretly hope for a sweet gift from a thoughtful partner. After all, wouldn't it be lovely to have someone who occasionally surprises them with a little token of care? And eventually, to have someone who walks through life with them, sharing all the ups and downs. This is where marriage becomes a beautiful chapter in a woman's life.

Becoming a mother is one of life's greatest joys for many women. They give of themselves in ways that no one else can—to bring new life into the world and nurture that life into adulthood. Through all the challenges, they become the heart of the home, ensuring that everyone feels cared for and supported. Their husband's and children's successes become their quiet victories. Meanwhile, the day-to-day responsibilities of making a living are, ideally, shared or shouldered by their partners.

As time goes on, something almost magical happens. The young woman who was once just another face in the crowd becomes a mother—radiant, confident, and full of grace. She blossoms into a woman whose beauty isn't just external but woven into the fabric of her spirit. There's a new glow, a depth, and charm that can't be described easily but is undeniably there.

This journey is different from that of women who find themselves still single after 30. There can be a tendency toward feeling a bit lonely or out of place, but that's when it's important to embrace life fully and keep the heart open. Avoiding love or companionship out of pride or fear can lead to unnecessary loneliness. Instead, women should be reminded of the incredible allure they possess—their inner and outer beauty is a gift to the world.

Women are artists of subtlety and charm. Sometimes they're shy and sweet, other times confident and bold. They know how to weave a dance of emotions, from playful to serious, teasing to sincere. And in that dance, they aren't just seeking love—they're offering it, with all its richness and joy.

Ultimately, it's not about being prey or predator. It's about finding connection, happiness, and living life with love and confidence.

## 50. WEIRD GUY

There's always that one weird guy who's just... different. You know the type—he prefers to be alone, doing things that make you wonder if he's lost the plot or if he's just a genius ahead of his time. Take his appearance, for example. One week, he's sporting a man bun like he's auditioning for a yoga commercial. The next, he's shaved his head completely bald, looking like a monk who just got kicked out of the monastery.

You might spot him walking around a park, or more likely, taking a *really* slow stroll around the lake, moving about a centimeter a minute. Maybe he's trying to promote environmental awareness or just practicing the art of doing absolutely nothing. When he's not on his ultra-slow walks, he's helping strangers with random acts of kindness, like pulling someone out of a pond because "the universe told him to."

He doesn't really have a steady job—his bank account is as unpredictable as his hairstyle. But somehow, he's always helping someone or raising money for a cause. Penniless? Sure. Generous? Absolutely. One day, he's organizing a charity drive for kids in the mountains; the next, he's squatting on the sidewalk, gnawing on a piece of street corn like it's his last meal. And yes, he'll talk about the universe while doing it—just don't expect the conversation to make sense.

This guy might be a frustrated artist, the type who calls a pile of trash in his living room a "contemporary art installation." His favorite subject to draw? The female form, of course, but in his own "artistic" style—big, bold, and full of what he calls "emotion" but what most people would just call, well... strange. Still, despite his wrinkled clothes and unkempt face, young women flock to him like he's some kind of hipster guru. Maybe it's the charm. Maybe it's the mystery. Or maybe it's just the free drinks he always seems to get.

When he's in the mood, he'll throw together some wild art show, the kind where half the people are there just to see what on earth he'll do next. Picture a gallery filled with haphazardly arranged objects, like an old TV on top of a bicycle wheel, all while he shouts something incomprehensible about "society's chains." And somehow, it draws a crowd—most of whom are there out of sheer curiosity, not because they understand anything that's going on.

In the end, he's harmless. A kind soul with a few loose screws, maybe, but undeniably lovable in his weird way. You can't help but smile when you see him, shaking your head, thinking, *"Only in America."*

## 51. PLANT STYLING

In various places—be it gardens just outside town, parks, or those abandoned cultural centers along the highway—you'll often come across potted plants with strange and sometimes downright baffling shapes. They seem to twist and bend as if the grower had a particularly peculiar vision—or maybe just a lot of time on their hands.

Here's the kicker: neither the grower nor the buyer likely has the slightest clue what these plants are supposed to represent. Some look like they've been contorted into knots, with roots so large they look like they've wrestled with the earth itself. Others resemble nature's version of a bad sci-fi movie, resembling twisting worms or leeches that might leap out at you if you get too close.

And yet, people pay good money for them.

Whenever I ask the sales clerk what a particular plant is meant to symbolize, I get one of two reactions. Either a pensive, deeply philosophical look, as if I've just asked them to ponder the mysteries of the universe, or they shoot me a glance that practically screams, *How dare you not know?* And then, in a tone dripping with seriousness, they'll say, "Ah, that's a flying dragon" or "Clearly, a dancing phoenix."

And I can't help but feel a little sympathy for the snobs who forked over a small fortune to buy these plants. They're out of pocket and don't even get an actual dragon for their trouble.

From what I've gathered, every plant is supposed to have its own spirit, its own story. Like the proud pine, standing tall and representing some heroic figure who's weathered life's storms and refuses to bow to the elements. Another pine might grow into a miniature mountain, symbolizing resilience and the determination to overcome any obstacle life throws your way. That's one pine, mind you. Then, you've got firs, cypresses, banyans, and figs—each contorted into some representation of the peculiar souls we meet in life.

But here's the real question: Do only a select few people have the proper credentials to "style" these plants into something meaningful? Or are we just getting more and more plants to sell to people who won't ask questions?

Because, let's face it, we all know a person like this in life. They're intelligent, mysterious, and their actions seem as unpredictable as the next twist in a bizarrely shaped bonsai. They talk big about world events, always with an air of importance, and seem to show up at the right gatherings, rubbing elbows with the right people.

But as time passes, the world changes, and you start to notice—they're still talking, but they've done surprisingly little. You look around at gatherings now, and no one really talks about them much anymore.

They've become like those fake miniature plants: once impressive, now just ornamental.

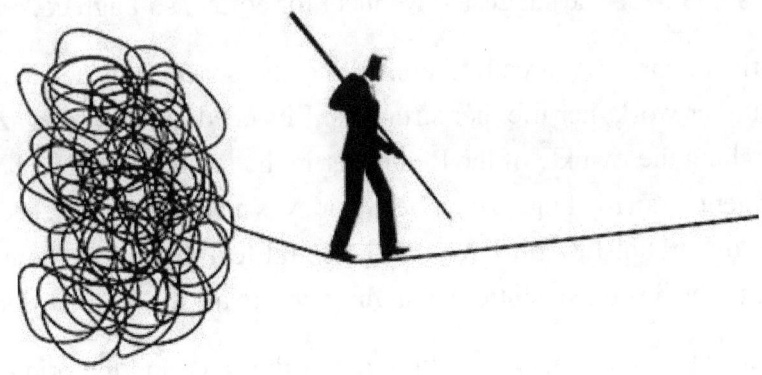

# 52. WHISPERS OF AUTUMN

## Sweetness

She smiled at me, a bit shy, standing there with her oversized suitcase. The afternoon light angled through the airplane doorway, warming her flushed cheeks. I greeted her, bent down to lift her bag into the overhead compartment, and caught her quiet gratitude in the sparkle of her eyes. I sat down next to her, half-hiding behind my newspaper but stealing glances. She was all warmth in the cold season.

When the plane landed, the evening sky had faded into a dusky gray. We walked side by side to the station. She moved quickly ahead, turning back just once to wave goodbye with that same, almost bashful smile. What lingered behind was her radiance, those eyes that glowed with gratitude, and the rhythm of her hips swaying in the chill air. I was thankful for that brief moment with her—a fleeting warmth on a winter's day.

## Flirting

We barely knew each other. Today, she called and mentioned how beautiful the autumn sunshine was. She suggested we meet for coffee, so I agreed.

When I arrived, she was already there, filling the space with her laughter and stories about her work, her life, her struggles. I listened quietly, my gaze drifting outside, catching the twinkle of the Red River in the fading light. Her hand found mine, and I gently ran my fingers over hers, our eyes meeting in a quiet connection. I didn't say much, but I didn't have to. She could feel that I was there with her, truly present. She hesitated, stuttering slightly before asking to sit closer.

Together, we sat by the window, looking out at the river and the bridges as they basked in the last of the day's light. She leaned into me, silent now, letting the moment carry us both. Then, with a start, she stood up, smiled, and said she felt safe around me—like she could say things she'd never dared to say before. She left abruptly, her glass of wine still half full.

## Autumn Afternoon

It's the end of autumn, and the wind dances lightly through the streets. The last rays of sunlight slip through the trees, sweeping up thin leaves in their final flutter. The air feels alive, like it has something gentle to whisper—something soft and sweet.

I sit beside her, a glass of red wine in hand, watching her as the day fades into evening. Her presence fills the space, and I know that just a few words would be all it would take for her to rest her head on my shoulder. But I keep quiet, letting the autumn breeze do the talking. It's as if the wind carries with it all the unspoken feelings between us, rustling through the leaves and filling the air with a quiet kind of magic.

Sometimes, silence speaks louder than words.

# 53. NEW ARCHITECTURE

Nature has this timeless beauty that always charms us, while man-made architecture, no matter how impressive it tries to be, often falls short. What do we get? Tubed, square buildings lined up like dominos, shooting up from the ground and squeezed together on small lots. Whether they're houses, schools, stations, offices, or the tangled intersections of rush hour, these structures can make us feel suffocated. No wonder we find ourselves fleeing to the outskirts on weekends or itching to travel even farther away.

Even the grandest buildings—palaces, mausoleums, or fancy luxury hotels—can't compete with nature's effortless splendor. Architecture, when you strip it down, is just a pile of bricks, stones, and mortar stacked together to shelter people from the rain and wind. It's more about function than beauty, more about utility than art. And in this modern world of steel and cement, things are getting worse. Buildings keep growing taller, higher, popping up everywhere in chaotic clumps, crowded and lonely at the same time. Inside, people huddle together like birds caught in a storm, all looking for shelter.

Sure, if you glance across the lake, you might catch the reflection of a sleek office building shimmering on the surface. It might even look beautiful for a second. But walk past it, sneak a glance over your shoulder, and suddenly, it's looming like a giant guillotine, casting a shadow that seems to follow you. You quicken your pace, feeling an odd chill run down your spine.

Every now and then, we stumble across architecture that actually gets it right—imitating nature and blending in gracefully. Take old pagodas, for example. Those moss-covered bricks, the ancient wood beams—everything about them feels harmonious with their surroundings. But, oh my, revisit that pagoda a few years later, and what do you find? The charming mossy bricks have been replaced by new ones, plastered with cement. Neat rows of plastic pipes snake under the roof where there used to be charm.

Old pagodas become new, and something beautiful slips away.

## 54. JOY OF LIFE

In my opinion, there are two main ways to find joy in life. One way is to surround ourselves with beauty—letting the environment we create bring us pleasure and comfort. The other way? It's to strip everything down and let that original, simple beauty shine through without the clutter.

Now, I've always leaned toward the latter approach. I've adopted a life principle: the less stuff around me, the better I feel. Every now and then, I go on a tidying spree, and if I hold something in my hand and realize it's no longer useful? Out it goes. It doesn't matter if it was a keepsake once—if it's collecting dust now, I either toss it or give it to someone else. Except for books. Books are sacred. They're the only things I keep close on this journey of life. Every time I pack up and move, you can be sure the books are coming with me.

The truth is, our surroundings have a huge impact on how we feel. The fewer objects we have around, the calmer we become. I swear, sometimes it feels like each item has its own little spirit—kind of like trees or people. And when there's too much stuff? All those *"spirits"* start creating chaos in our heads.

But when you clear away the clutter, something magical happens. You start to see the true beauty in the things you've chosen to keep. You can finally appreciate the simple moments—the sunrise greeting you every morning, the birds chirping away in the garden, or that twilight glow as the sun peeks through the trees. Even the sound of crickets in the evening becomes something comforting and sweet.

In the end, life's simple pleasures don't need much dressing up. They're just waiting for us to notice them.

233

## 55. PRIVATE SHELTER

People's true personalities really shine when they're off the clock, lounging at home, free from the daily grind. When they're not hustling for a paycheck, chasing fame, or juggling endless responsibilities, that's when you see who they really are. Work life can be a battlefield, full of politics, strategy, and, let's face it, a bit of self-interest. So, judging someone based on their workplace behavior is often unfair. You might have a bossy executive who's actually a great neighbor, or a cutthroat businessperson who's a doting parent and a loving spouse.

We all live with at least two, maybe more, versions of ourselves. One version is the problem-solver who deals with the outside world, and the other is the homebody who enjoys life in private. Think of it like this: your living room is always on display, but your bedroom? That's a whole other story. And let's not forget, every house has a few hidden rooms no one ever talks about.

Home is where you get to be your truest self, where you can kick back and let your secret quirks out. It's your personal shelter, your sanctuary. Home should be the place where you live the most authentically, where you can let down your guard and embrace your own rhythms.

This is why the way we decorate our homes matters. It's not about cluttering up the space with random stuff. No, your home should have only what's essential—a place for everything and everything in its place. Keep it simple, keep it meaningful. That's where the magic of home happens.

## 56. MOTHER AND LESSONS

### Flowers for Mother

On Teacher's Day, I found myself carrying the most beautiful bunch of flowers, but instead of delivering them to a classroom, I took them to my mother.

As always, my parents sat together in those familiar chairs, waiting. My mother, as usual, greeted me with warm hands and a few questions. It had been a long time since her students visited. Most of them had flown off to some distant sky, possibly never to return.

Perhaps, in some small way, I was her only student who came back.

You know, it would be wonderful if there were a Teacher's Day every month. I'd be sure to bring her flowers each time. But to my surprise, she didn't even glance at the bouquet I brought. No, her eyes were more interested in holding my hands. It was as if, at that moment, I was the most important lesson she needed.

### Classroom Teaching

I've always loved teaching in the classroom—it's exhilarating, really. Sure, it requires preparation and lots of reading, but the best part is distilling complex ideas into something simple, something that clicks for the students. In the process, I find myself learning too.

The classroom? It's a whole universe of stories. Every student brings a new perspective, a fresh take on life. And, because it's a group setting, you're compelled to communicate in a way that's both thoughtful and engaging. You end up learning not just the material, but also how to reach people where they are.

Teaching has given me so much: new knowledge, a sense of purpose, and a chance to ignite that same curiosity in others. I often wonder, what will I leave behind in this world? My legacy might just be in the form of those students who grew into their potential. Some thrived, some stumbled, but they all kept moving forward.

Every now and then, one of them reaches out to call me "teacher." And in that moment, I realize—that's joy.

## 57. SOUND OF TIME

I'm sitting in a quiet room, and suddenly my thoughts pause. That's when I notice the ever-present hum of the modern world—the buzz of machines, air conditioners, fans, and even lightbulbs. It's like the universe's own white noise soundtrack, just a steady, unremarkable hum in the background of life.

Out in nature, though, it's different. There, the sounds shift with the wind rustling through the trees, the crack of distant thunder, or the rhythmic crash of waves against the shore. Once, I visited the North Mountain. I trekked across mountain passes, fields, and winding roads that snaked past houses nestled deep in the landscape. The world felt ancient and endless.

My country's history stretches over 4,000 years—impressive, though it pales next to the grand timeline of the Earth, which has seen billions of years roll by. Whole civilizations have risen and crumbled in the blink of geological time. Meanwhile, here we are, scrambling around for our few short decades, worrying about the next project, the next deadline, the next success.

When I reached the Northern Village Falls, the roar of the thick, silver water was all I could hear. The waterfall rushed down, drenching everything in its path with spray, and in that endless blur of water, I thought I could almost hear time itself whispering. It reminded me of my history, my ancestors, the brevity of life, and all the big dreams still left unfinished.

And then I realized: maybe instead of worrying so much, we should just listen to the sound of time. Let it remind us that while our lives may be short, they don't need to be rushed. There's wisdom in slowing down and thinking deeply.

Time hums along, regardless. We might as well enjoy the tune.

## 58. GOODBYE OLD YEAR

It was close to midnight, the sky tinted with a strange pink hue. Maybe it was the glow from the street lamps or the lingering reflection of some unfinished construction. With only a few days left before the new year, I found myself thinking about everything I'd done—or more accurately, hadn't done—over the past year.

Everything was pretty average, nothing to write home about. A few projects that never really took off, still being pushed and pulled by some ex-colleagues. One or two companies went under, and I received a handful of letters from disgruntled employees—apparently, their directors weren't exactly role models.

There were a couple of fresh projects that sparked my interest, and I met a few new faces. Some of the old, reliable ones fell from grace—typical, right? The papers were full of economic chatter, claiming prospects were decent, though credit growth lagged behind. Parliament had its usual chaotic sessions, and a vote of confidence took center stage, as it always does. Some people were thrilled; others couldn't care less. The usual mix.

As for me, I tried—really tried—to live a little more quietly this year. After a few rowdy nights where I drank too much and did some embarrassingly stupid things, I made a promise to myself: fewer drinks, fewer distractions. That lasted until autumn, of course. Then the emptiness hit, and I found myself reconnecting with old friends over a few casual drinks. So much for resolutions.

My health? Not bad. I stuck to morning exercise routines, except on business trip days or after those regrettable nights of drinking. Food became simpler—mostly veggies. I lost some weight, became thinner. Sometimes I'd catch myself in the mirror and see a familiar stranger staring back. Vague eyes, a tired expression—I was almost unrecognizable to myself. Thoughts of mortality crept in, especially when I heard about friends passing. I dusted off my will, opened it, then closed it again. Maybe I'd update it. Maybe I wouldn't.

But this year wasn't all doom and gloom. I took a memorable trip, scaling a few mountain peaks, learning more about myself—and humanity in general—along the way. Bought more books, of course. Dove into some love stories with philosophical undertones, which were surprisingly comforting. Finished a few meditation lectures, upped my exercise game, and even spent time with two or

237

three revered monks. For a brief moment, I nearly became the deputy abbot at an old pagoda. I envisioned a life of morning meditation, afternoon reading, and peaceful evenings. But, as life often goes, something happened, and the mountains had to wait.

On the love front, things entered a quieter, more peaceful phase. No more rush or noise. Love became softer, sweeter—like a secret road leading to freedom. I'd grown tired of all the heat and intensity. These days, it's more about taking my time, breathing deeply, and savoring the simple pleasures.

And just like that, another year is about to drift away. We come, we go. We meet, we part. We stop, we start again. Slowly.

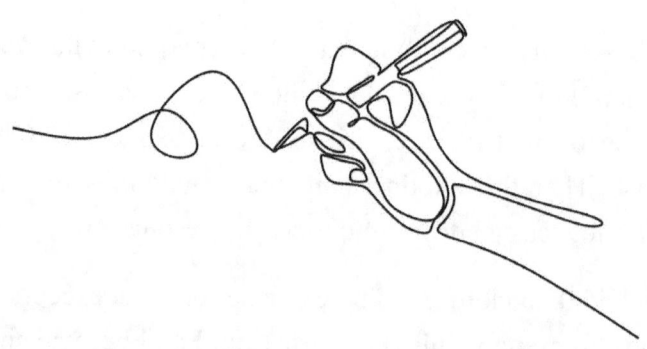

## 59. LOST

I've lost something. It's that slippery feeling that comes and goes, like a passing shadow on a sunny day. I can't quite put my finger on it, but there it is—a flicker of something familiar that feels just out of reach.

I get this feeling when I stumble across an old book, or when I walk down a street I haven't been to in years, or even when I catch a glimpse of someone who looks vaguely familiar. It reminds me of...someone, something. It's like I've been here before, but I can't remember when or why.

In the rush of everyday life, these little emotions flash by so quickly, I barely have time to grab hold of them before they're gone. And yet, when they come, they leave a tiny pang—a feeling that something important has slipped away. Not enough to break your heart, but just enough to make you wonder.

It's a bit like an autumn breeze brushing against your cheek—so soft it could almost be a dream, and then it's gone. The past has a way of doing that: brushing up against you when you least expect it, leaving only hints and glimmers of the moments you thought you'd forgotten.

Sometimes, I look back at those moments, and I think about the things that didn't quite pan out. Like that time I seriously considered becoming a monk, wandering off into the wilderness for some deep, quiet isolation. It seemed like the right thing to do back then. Or the lover I was certain was going to change my life—an ideal that seemed so real in my head but never quite materialized in reality.

I guess those little losses are just old dreams, summoned from the shadows of time. They come up quietly, whispering of what could have been, and then, like the wind, they disappear again.

## 60. BOOK OF MY LIFE

I've carefully planned out everything I shouldn't do—and everything I should—with all the passion and good intentions one can muster. I call it *The Book of My Life*. It's simple, really: exercise every morning, spend more time having dinner with my kids, read daily, only make love with the woman I love, and visit my parents weekly. Sounds easy, right? Well, in theory.

In my book, I speak about saying no to smoking cigars (as satisfying as they may be), drinking no more than two glasses of wine at a time (though a third has a way of sneaking in), avoiding being too sweet or flirting with young women (because who needs the complication?), and traveling at least once a year (to escape the everyday chaos). Every few years, I even plan to retreat into nature—just me, the mountains, and some peace and quiet. It's a bit of a reset for the mind and body, something like a spiritual detox.

I've also added a chapter on leadership—controlling my temper, listening more, never getting angry with my staff. Providing them with a comfortable work environment and better pay seems like a win-win. I even planned on acting with more thoughtfulness around old friends, remembering to drink good wine with a few soul mates once or twice a year for the sheer joy of it.

It all sounds so simple, doesn't it? Yet, as life tends to do, things get complicated. Sometimes, I open the book, read a few lines, and laugh at the sheer optimism of it all. Somehow, a cigar still finds its way into my hand, and two glasses of wine? Well, let's just say that's a suggestion, not a rule.

But that's life, right? The balance between intention and reality, between lofty goals and the inevitable detours. Still, it's all there in my book—plans, hopes, the occasional slip-ups. And even when I stray from the script, I find myself turning back to those pages, reading a few lines, and smiling.

Because, in the end, life is lovely—chaos and all.

## 61. VEGETARIAN DIET

Every now and then, when I visit a pagoda or a vegetarian restaurant, I'm always intrigued by the variety of vegan dishes that somehow look just like meat. There's faux fish, imitation sausage, even pretend crab and fake eggs. You have to wonder—why does meat still hold such a powerful grip on us?

Even for monks, or regular people like myself who try to live a healthier, more mindful life, there's always this desire for "normal" meals. But does "normal" mean food that's shaped like meat, even if it isn't? Do we think it tastes better just because it looks familiar? Maybe for Mahayana monks, who don't just practice Buddhism for themselves but also aim to guide others, these mock-meat dishes help them stay connected to the everyday people they serve. Perhaps for those of us trying to dip a toe into the vegan world without fully renouncing our carnivorous tendencies, this faux meat bridges the gap and makes us feel a little more...normal? I'm not sure what everyone's thinking when they go vegan, but I have my theories.

As for me, I find that keeping it simple is often best. A small bowl of rice, some vegetables like carrots or turnips sliced thin and stir-fried just right, a little tofu sautéed with spring onions, and maybe a handful of roasted peanuts. Add a dash of soy sauce and pepper if you want a little kick. Chew slowly, savor each bite, and before long you'll notice that you feel lighter, calmer, and maybe even a bit more serene. Your whole outlook changes—your mind clears, and surprisingly, even your desires shift. That constant craving for more—more food, more pleasure—starts to fade. You still have desires, of course, but they're more...refined.

And here's the funny part. You find that even as your cravings decrease, suddenly you're the one catching people's eyes! There's a new sparkle in your gaze, a sort of quiet charm that draws people in. Maybe it's the peace in your aura, or maybe women just like the idea of a man who's more...vegetarian? It's a strange twist—am I their favorite dish now? Vegan with a side of mystery? How perplexing!

I've always had a soft spot for Mahayana Buddhism, and I like to think I'm a Buddhist who appreciates other perspectives too. Is there some magic formula where we can enjoy the pleasures of life—yes, even lust—and still keep that vegan virtue? Wouldn't that be ideal?

It reminds me of my childhood. I used to love playing in the rain. When summer

241

arrived, and the skies opened up with a cool, refreshing downpour, all the kids would run into the streets, arms wide open, shouting with joy. It was the best feeling—until our parents decided we might catch a cold. Suddenly, we had to wear raincoats, hats, or even stay indoors. It wasn't quite the same, but we found a way to have fun anyway.

Maybe this is the lesson: why not throw on a metaphorical raincoat, open your arms wide, and sing in the rain? If meat could be vegan, wouldn't that be a refreshing twist? Perhaps, in the eyes of the devout, I'm a vegan dish pretending to be meat. But to me, maybe I'm a meat dish masquerading as vegan. Either way, it's pretty tasty.

## 62. WIND OF CHANGE

The last days of autumn are slipping away, like the final scenes of a movie where everything lingers for just a moment longer. The air feels like it's holding its breath, waiting. It's one of those sunny days where the sky is a clear, endless blue, but there's a thin gold shimmer coating everything—almost like nature itself is putting on a filter.

Tall trees stand guard over the roads, while cars and people flow beneath them. A cool breeze snakes through the branches, giving the lake a gentle ripple. A few leaves drift lazily on the surface, as if they're in no rush to reach the shore. Every now and then, a carp breaks the surface, glancing up at the sky as if it too is pondering the change in seasons.

There's a persistent wind in the air now, rustling the leaves, making the few little purple flowers on the garden wall tremble. The bell hanging nearby starts to chime softly in the distance, its sound carried by the wind. Soon, it rings louder, a bit more insistent. Even the fruit—apples, pears, grapes, and dragon fruit on the table— seem to glow brighter under the autumn light. It's as though nature is trying to tell me something. Maybe something new is just around the corner.

Inside, a group of ascetics dressed in their dark brown robes move quietly through the house. Their steps are so soft, it feels as if they're gliding, barely touching the ground. My family has been hosting them since their long pilgrimage last month. They've brought with them a sense of calm, as though even time itself slows down when they are near.

Is the wind saying its farewells to autumn? Or maybe the bell is ringing to greet something—or someone—new. I can't quite tell. One thing's for sure: my house feels less like a home today and more like a monastery.

Maybe that's what happens when the wind of change blows through—you start to see the world a little differently, even your own space. Perhaps the monks aren't the only ones on a journey.

## 63. LUSTFUL GUYS

I'm a serious man—at least that's what everyone says. Especially my staff. I work hard and play hard, but I keep those two worlds separate. Mostly.

But then there's this friend of mine, and honestly, he makes me question myself sometimes. He's always hanging around, right behind me, following my every move. On the surface, he's a gentleman. Polite, quick to catch on—he's the kind of guy who pulls out chairs for women, holds doors open, and helps them out of their coats with this perfectly timed grace. You'd think he's some kind of sensitive mind reader, because he can take one look at me and immediately know what I need.

But—and here's the kicker—he has this embarrassing side. He gets me into the most awkward situations without a second thought. He's eager to please, but sometimes, he's downright impulsive. Picture this: we're at a party, and out of nowhere, he's scooping up a girl, spinning her around like she's a prize he's just won. The poor thing is so startled she ends up hugging me for dear life. And where am I? Mortified. Meanwhile, he's still at it—holding, touching, caressing, like we're in some kind of romance novel. It's honestly disgusting.

And yet, women—well, some women—are strangely charmed by him. Instead of pushing him away, they laugh, blush, and adjust their hair, or brush off imaginary dust from their lapels like they're flattered. It's madness. I should be lecturing him on boundaries, but then I'm the one who gets the side-eye.

Worst of all is when I've had a few too many drinks. That's when he really lets loose. No sense of decorum. He's off on his own, ignoring me completely and doing whatever he pleases. And I'll tell you this—he's got a twin brother who's just as mischievous, always ready to join in the fun. They're in cahoots, these two. It's like they take turns causing trouble, and I'm left to deal with the aftermath.

So, who are these two partners in crime? My hands. Those lustful guys. I swear, I'm innocent! At least, that's what I told myself this morning when I woke up after a long night of drinking. But honestly, with friends like these, who needs enemies?

## 64. WORK

Humans are born to work, plain and simple. Even playing, eating, resting, and, yes, even making love—all fall under the banner of work if you think about it. It's just another performance of our duties. You can't escape it. Work is the great connector between your body, soul, nature, and, somehow, the cosmos. So, you work to live, and in some strange twist, you also live to work.

Work requires sweat, persistence, and the willingness to tackle the same mistakes over and over, just to see if you learn something new. And sometimes, knowing it's a mistake doesn't stop you from repeating it because, let's face it, we're only human.

The thing about work is it often follows a strict routine—it can be dull, repetitive, and, let's be honest, a little soul-sucking at times. Someone once said that when you work with love, you're in heaven, and when you work without it, you're in hell. Well, if that's true, I'd say we're all shuttling between heaven and hell more often than we'd like to admit. Perhaps we even spend more time on the fiery side of things.

When passion's missing, work gets stuck in the shadows. You make nothing of worth, not even to yourself. Passion is the spark, the creative force that breathes life into your work, making it more than just a task—making it meaningful. That's when your work gets your personal stamp, and the magic happens.

And whether it's work or play, dedication is key. Really think about it: nothing worth doing comes without a little sweat and a lot of prep. That's what makes the effort worth it—and the enjoyment that much sweeter.

So, I think the trick is to work with love and love with energy. Mornings for practicing, afternoons for working, and evenings for loving—that sounds like an ideal daily schedule, right?

It's simple. Easy to understand. But, oh boy, is it hard to follow.

# 65. WINE

People have written countless pages on wine—how to drink it, savor it, pair it, you name it. You'd think it was the art of alchemy or some noble industry that requires a Ph.D. in viniculture. But really, drinking wine is like anything else—it can be simple, fun, and it doesn't have to drain your wallet.

The secret to enjoying wine? It's all about finding the right bottle to match your mood. Feeling introspective? Grab a bottle of red with some age on it, one that has that deep, oaky scent mixed with a hint of tobacco or coffee. Sip it slowly, and you'll find yourself sinking into your thoughts like you've just stumbled on a great mystery novel.

When you're with friends, well, that's where it gets interesting. Depending on the crowd, their personalities, and what's on the menu, you've got to decide whether to go with something sharp or soft, light or strong. And if you're hosting a party, there's an unspoken rule: you need at least three types of wine—white, something sweet and golden, and a red that runs from light to deep. Think of each bottle as a musical note. You need at least two or three notes to compose a decent tune.

And here's a pro tip: if you've selected the wines ahead of time, make a little show out of it. Each time you pop a cork, introduce the wine to your guests like it's an old friend. Describe its quirks, its flavors, and why you thought it would be the perfect guest at your table tonight.

Not only does this elevate the wine's importance, but it also makes the party feel warmer, more connected, and a little more intimate.

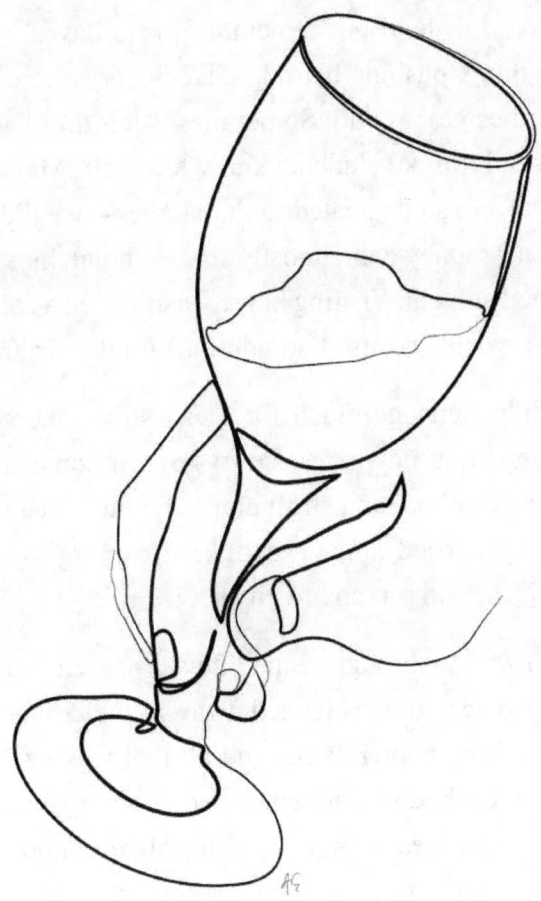

## 66. MEMORY

I went back to visit my old school on the last summer day, dragging my kids along with me. Walking through the quiet corridors, I passed by a few people, ghosted past the closed auditoriums and dusty labs, and finally arrived at the Faculty where I'd studied thirty years before. It felt like a time capsule with unfamiliar faces and a few old photos on the wall—maybe it was the summer lull, or maybe it was just the long years between me and my youth playing tricks on me.

As we walked, I couldn't help but remember those days. I was always full of energy, trying everything, pushing hard. I walked everywhere back then, wearing the same ragged clothes year-round. Sometimes, I felt the sharp sting of poverty, that embarrassment only broke students know too well. Maybe that's why all of us overseas students were so dedicated to our studies—we didn't have much, but we had that drive. Our money came mostly from scholarships and the occasional bonus for being a good student. Visiting home wasn't even a consideration; I didn't see my family for six years because I couldn't afford the airfare.

Summer holidays didn't change much for me; I still wandered into the library because, frankly, there was nowhere else to go. On some days, when the sun was just right, I'd leave school and stroll along the busy main avenue, following beautiful girls as they hurried along, sunlight streaming through their skirts. I walked like that until the sun set, and reality set in.

The road to the dorm wound through a small flower garden. During the summer or autumn afternoons, I'd see couples tucked away in the corners, whispering their secrets to each other. Then winter came, and all that was left were cold benches occupied by lonely men huddled together for warmth, their tattered coats no match for the biting cold. By early morning, I'd walk to school and see those same benches, now covered with snow, like statues frozen in time. The entire garden turned into a snow-white wonderland.

I still remember the first time I saw snow through the glass of the auditorium window. The snowflakes whirled around, carried by the wind. It moved me so deeply that I wrote a poem right then and there—about missing home, missing my family. I sent it to my girlfriend, who was thousands of miles away.

Six months later, I received a small envelope. Excited, I tore it open, only to find a few blank pages with faint water stains and a single line: *"Missed you too."*

Another time, at the end of summer, I met a beautiful girl visiting from another city. We had a few happy days together before she disappeared without a word. I spent my days sitting by a small stream near the dorm, watching leaves float by, scribbling out long, wistful poems to her. After months of waiting, I finally received a Telex telling me to visit her immediately. And just like that, a bittersweet love story full of tears began.

But that's all in the past now. As I watched my kids laughing and playing, I couldn't help but wonder what roads they'll travel. Their lives are just beginning, and though they'll walk different paths, I can't help but smile, knowing that they too will have their own stories to tell someday.

# 67. MISTAKES AND REGRETS

## *Making Mistakes*

Building and developing an organization requires wisdom, loyalty, and discipline. At first, it's all about getting those basics right—finding the sharp minds, enforcing the rules, and hoping everyone has enough sense to stay loyal. But as the organization grows, things get trickier. You need even more wisdom, new blood, and you start worrying less about loyalty and more about who's going to stab you in the back when you're not looking.

The more wisdom you gain, the more contradictions you create inside yourself. Your ego gets bruised, and it stings. True loyalty? Well, that's a rare bird. Instead of loyal folks, you end up surrounded by sycophants who'll nod along to anything you say, even if it's nonsense. You tighten discipline, and suddenly, you've got a bunch of robots—dull, slow, and just following orders.

And there you are, at the center of it all, feeling like a dictator, but instead of a crown, you've got headaches. The organization, just like a living being, needs something deeper—beliefs, values, a reason to exist beyond making spreadsheets and meeting quotas. Without these, your organization starts crumbling as soon as you walk away.

It's no different from leading a country. Every leader, from CEOs to presidents, ends up reading about history and realizing one thing: They're just a collection of mistakes waiting to happen.

## *Regret*

At some point, you're going to cause someone pain. Maybe you've already done it, or maybe it's coming down the road, but rest assured, it's inevitable. Sometimes, it's because you're young and clueless, other times, it's because success went to your head, and you couldn't see your own faults. You've hurt people—enemies, friends, colleagues, family—and sometimes, you didn't even mean to. Other times, you had to be charming and diplomatic for the sake of a deal, then you went home and acted like a complete jerk to the ones closest to you. Why? Because the mask came off.

It's unforgivable, really. And if someone ever does point out your flaws, you probably ignore them. Maybe you even face backlash, or revenge, but the mistakes keep coming. Apologizing? That's tough, especially when the damage is already done, and there's no one left to apologize to.

That's the moment it hits you: regret. You realize you couldn't have done it any other way, even if you wanted to. And all that's left to do is let out a sigh, full of all the things you didn't fix in time.

I've been there. I felt the regret, told myself I'd change, and promised I'd clear my mind for the future. But change takes time—and even more mistakes.

## 68. ATTACHED

Young women are a delightful puzzle. At first, they crave tenderness and attention. Then, they gently escalate things into needing care—a lot of care. They're sensitive, thoughtful, and have the unique ability to throw you completely off-kilter with a single tear. The thing is, they're refreshingly honest with their emotions, while we, men, tend to bottle things up. They often say they're fragile, but honestly, I think I'm the fragile one. I just don't admit it out loud.

They're practical too. They observe, compare, and slowly—very slowly—pull you into their orbit with that silent, expectant look that says, "Are you paying attention?" They never say it, but somehow, you're always on the hook.

What do we want from them? It's simple yet complicated. We want their sweetness, their allure—sometimes, we just need a bit of sympathy or someone who gets it. And let's be honest, we love their bodies, the way they move so effortlessly, their gracefulness that can make you feel ecstatic with a mere glance.

But then, we want their faith. We want them to trust us. Except, we forget that with faith comes responsibility—a lot of it. And the weight of all that responsibility? It's heavy. Too heavy sometimes.

I try to think of them as my close companions, people I guide and encourage along the way. A shared path for a while, a hand to hold, someone to laugh with. And when they decide to move on—whether that's down a different path or to someone else—I remind myself not to make them sad. Be kind. Be gentle. If I can, show them I care.

A message, a question, a small gift now and then—it's the little things. I guess, in the end, I'm still attached. Aren't we all?

## 69. TEACHER

My teacher was a very strict person. Solving any problem raised by him required great effort, hard work, and often an uncomfortably long time. If luck was on your side, a project might be completed in a few months, but often it took years. We were foreign students, and time wasn't a luxury we could afford. Instead of studying 8-10 hours a day, we'd sometimes push ourselves to work 20 hours a day, for months at a time. With sheer willpower (and a bit of sleep deprivation), we could speed up the process.

I remember the joy of finally bringing my report to him, hoping it might make its way into a scientific journal. But, oh Lord! Writing that long article—although its core content was only a few pages—took months, sometimes a year. Crafting the correct scientific words, formulas, and carefully annotating the results was one thing; editing the vocabulary and structuring the sentences to be perfectly unambiguous was another. It was pure misery! At the time, I blamed him for the relentless perfectionism, but now I understand.

Beneath his cold and harsh exterior was a deeply thoughtful and emotional man. One time, in my youthful ignorance, I sent my research findings to some other famous scientists, hoping for quicker recognition. My teacher discovered this, and for the next three years, he seemed to watch me struggle from a distance, paying me little attention. I felt as if I were swimming in an ocean of hopelessness, even though I was still solving problems. By my final undergraduate year, I was so lost that I considered asking for a transfer to another field of study. I thought I'd never have the chance to pursue my postgraduate dreams.

Then, five months before graduation, he called me into his office. To my surprise, he had already prepared all the documents for me to stay on as a postgraduate student. It turned out he had been silently watching over me all along, pushing me to grow. A year later, I completed my Ph.D. and returned to my home country. He visited me a few times, urging me to return and continue my research. I promised I'd return in a year or two. But 25 years have passed, and I haven't gone back. Life, as they say, has its way.

Every few years, I visit him, and every time, I'm reminded of his gentle nature beneath that stern exterior. Whenever we meet or say goodbye at the airport, he never hides his tears. The image of him with his gray hair and faded suit, bending down to dry the tears rolling down his cheeks with a handkerchief, is etched in my mind.

As my birthday approaches each year, without fail, I receive a call from him, with his kind and heartfelt wishes. When we reunite, we often share a bottle of wine and talk like old friends. He's not just a great scientist—he's well-versed in literature, art, and history. His opinions are always refined, thoughtful, and occasionally, delightfully surprising. He embodies the traditional values of his culture, working tirelessly even in his seventies. If he's not giving a lecture or attending a conference, he's at the Institute, even on Saturdays. When I asked him why he never left for a more prosperous country with better working conditions like many of his colleagues, he simply replied, *"My love is here, in my homeland. I don't need to go anywhere."*

He's often quiet, more of a listener, but when asked for his thoughts, his comments are profound. And while he adores beauty, he never lets himself gaze too long at an unfamiliar beautiful woman—a discipline I've yet to master. I'm forever grateful to my teacher and his country. They not only nurtured me in my younger years but also shaped me into who I am today.

I've learned so much from my teacher—though, I admit, there are still a few lessons that escape me. New knowledge excites me, but so does the allure of a beautiful woman. I tell myself that, with a bit more time and maturity, perhaps after my 50th birthday, I'll learn to curb my curiosity—or at least indulge it in a more discreet manner.

## 70. WORDS OF LOVE (I)

My parents loved their children fiercely, though they had their own unique way of showing it. I vividly recall the days leading up to Tet, when they'd work tirelessly through the night. The steady rhythm of the sewing machine felt almost eternal— tick, tick, tick—like it had made some secret pact with the moon. Morning would come, and there they were, still working as if the night had been a mere pause, not a break. That image, so full of effort and care, is burned into my memory.

My father, well, let's just say "strict" doesn't quite do him justice. He carried the weight of our family on his broad shoulders, but his one real wish was for us to study hard and grow into decent people. Yet when I think of him, it's not just his love that comes to mind—there are also flashes of those terrifying beatings and the overly creative punishments for when I spent more time playing than studying. If I bring it up now, though, he'll brush it off with a laugh. "That's impossible!" he'll say. "I loved you too much for that." And you know what? I believe him. He really did love us, even if his version of affection came with a little more "tough" than "love." Beneath that stern exterior, he was a softie, too. I once stumbled upon some old notes from his time studying abroad, and—surprise, surprise—they were full of romantic musings. Who knew? Yet, even after discovering that side of him, I still craved his words of love spoken out loud.

Now, my mother, she was the sweet, quiet one. Steady as the sun, always making sure everyone was cared for. I remember sitting behind her on her old bicycle one day when my foot got caught in the spokes. It was just a little scratch, but she scolded me with all the concern of a mother whose heart had taken the hit, not my ankle. And then there was the time I brought home good grades. She had saved up just enough money to take me to the shop for new shoes. I'll never forget the way her face lit up as I tried them on. That, right there, was one of the happiest moments of my life.

Now, decades later, after studying abroad, establishing a career, and finding my way in life, I often think back. Even on my busiest days, filled with work, meetings, teaching, or the occasional wine party with friends, I find myself growing quiet. I've learned to sit back and muse, to reflect on the moments that truly shaped me—those small, quiet gestures of love that spoke louder than any words could.

One day, I visited my parents. We sat in the garden, surrounded by the familiar hum of life—trees swaying gently in the breeze, sunshine streaming through the leaves like an old friend visiting after a storm. We talked for hours, about nothing in particular and everything at once. And suddenly, as I watched them smiling in the light, I thought to myself, *Time moves so fast. What will happen to this scene, to these people?*

I realized then that no matter how busy life gets, no matter how many meetings or deadlines demand my attention, I need to make more time for these moments. To sit with them, talk with them, to simply *be* with them. If I'm busy, I'll make sure my wife and children visit them, too—to share in the joy of these fleeting, beautiful days. Because one day, the garden may be quiet without them, and I want to hold on to every whisper of love while I still can.

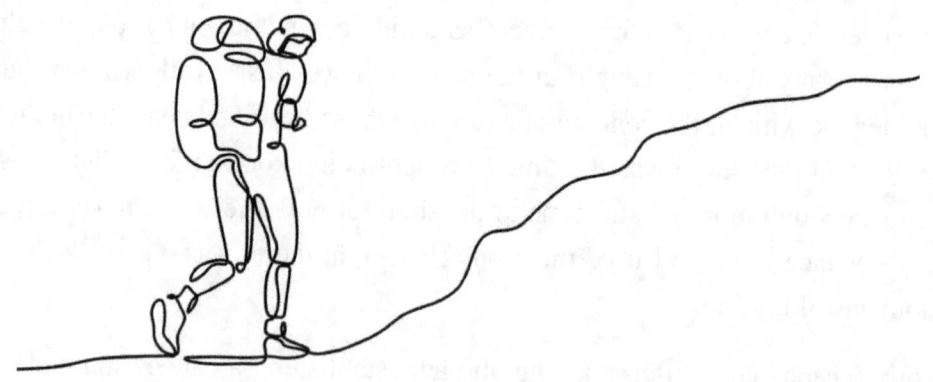

## 71. WORDS OF LOVE (II)

My children are grown now, each with their own unique quirks. My oldest son—he's quiet, with a head of fluffy hair that always seems to be slightly out of place. His gaze is often off somewhere in the distance, as if he's pondering the mysteries of the universe. My youngest daughter, on the other hand, is sharp as a tack, always observing me with a calculating eye. She loves fiercely but can also hate just as passionately. Then there's my eldest daughter—beautiful and full of energy, always bubbling with excitement about her next big plan or a new friend she's made. And my youngest son, well, he's the most innocent of them all. Sometimes he'll call me up just to say how much he misses me, and it absolutely melts my heart. But when we're face-to-face, all he ever seems to ask for is food or toys!

I've come to accept that each of them has their own little world. They're carving their own paths in life, as they should. We bring them into the world, shape their childhoods, but their souls and fates? Those are entirely their own. We pour love into them, but we can't steer their ships.

Still, I can't help but want them to remember me—not just for the food, toys, or the lectures about life—but for the love I've tried to show them. Before long, they'll be off on their own, fully absorbed in their journeys. So, whenever I can, I hug them, touch their hair, kiss their cheeks, and whisper how much I love them. Even if they squirm a little.

Yesterday, during our year-end family gathering, my wife, who's a firm believer in reincarnation, leaned over and whispered to me, *"You know, in a past life, I was probably your daughter."* I just chuckled. But it did make me realize that with all the busyness of life, I hadn't said any words of love to her in a while.

So, I made a little promise to myself: From now on, I'm going to remember to say those loving words—especially to the eldest daughter from my past life. Better not disappoint her in this one.

## 72. WORDS OF LOVE (III)

Rarely could I corral all of my kids to gather at my house. They'd either be racing around the garden like wild creatures or huddled together, gossiping and playing games in some hidden corner. Meanwhile, I'd be in the kitchen, cooking with all the attentiveness of a five-star chef. Of course, my youngest son would sneak in repeatedly, asking if the food was ready yet. I must've told him to scram at least a dozen times.

Finally, when everything was perfectly prepared, I called them all to the table. Watching them eat, I couldn't help but proudly introduce each dish like I was hosting a cooking show. They listened, sort of.

They ate quickly, chatting and laughing about who knows what. They exchanged knowing winks like they were in on some secret. My eldest daughter gave me a sly nod, *"Tasty meat, Dad, but just a bit chewy, don't you think?"* My youngest daughter grinned, *"The stir-fried veggies are crispy, Daddy, yummy!"* My son, always the diplomat, reassured me, *"Don't worry, we'll do the dishes after we finish."* And my youngest? He was too focused on shoveling food into his mouth to bother with chewing. I didn't think I saw him chew once.

After the meal, I slipped out to the garden to check on the flowers and watch the goldfish glide through the pond. From the kitchen, I heard the distant clinks of bowls, muffled laughter, and the hum of their conversation. Then, suddenly, from behind me, my eldest son called out, *"Dad, your fried rice was excellent! Can you make it again next time?"* I barely had time to answer before he grabbed my hands, grinned with his big belly full, and his eyes twinkling with mischief.

He spun around, bursting with energy, and began prancing around the garden, singing, *"Pretty butterfly, pretty butterfly, an amarous one..."*

Ah, kids. Always full of surprises.

## 73. DRUNK MOSQUITO

No sensation is quite as delightful as when you're on the edge of being drunk. It's an indescribable state of joy, happiness, and excitement that feels like pure magic. Suddenly, you become a completely different person.

What was once a tedious day with boring tasks, tiresome faces, and endless worries now feels lighter, like everything is unstuck and moving again. After a few glasses of wine, the world looks brighter. You start laughing, sharing stories, and even your eyes light up, seeing beauty in every little thing. You might make a few reckless but harmless gestures—innocent, even charming. Nothing seems ugly or annoying anymore.

Wine really is a little miracle. It's like nature's way of letting you tap into something divine. What more could you ask for in life? There are tough, exhausting days. Moments of deep thought or restless nights. Lonely hours when the world feels heavy. And then, there are nights like tonight—when you feel infatuated, alive, and just a little tipsy. You're living the whole spectrum, experiencing it all.

Tonight, we drank. My friend flew thousands of miles just to be here. It had been forever since we last saw each other. We started out sitting across the table, toasting like old pals. Before we knew it, we were hugging, laughing, and pouring more wine. How good it felt! We reminisced about the old days, talked about random nonsense, and planned for adventures that we knew we'd never take. We agreed on just one bottle but ended up finishing four—each one drained to the last drop.

Afterward, I took him out to the garden to admire the shimmering lake. The night was still, and everything felt just right—until I felt a little sting on my wrist. I looked down and saw a fat, sluggish mosquito with a belly full of, well, probably me. It flapped its wings awkwardly, tried to fly but kept wobbling and landing on my shirt, then bouncing off to the seat beside me.

For some reason, I decided not to kill it. It just seemed... weird. Like it had lost its way.

And then I realized—it wasn't just me who had too much to drink. That mosquito was drunk!

I had to laugh. There it was, a tiny little drunk mosquito, struggling to keep it together, just like the rest of us sometimes. My friend, half asleep by now, leaned on my shoulder, breathing softly. We both sat there, under the stars, with a drunk mosquito for company. And I felt a strange sort of comfort in that.

Really, life is full of surprises. Even tiny drunk ones.

## 74. GOD

In moments of joy or sorrow, we often find ourselves calling on God. Whether we're overjoyed or downcast, He seems to linger at the edge of our thoughts—close enough to feel like a companion, yet distant enough to remain a mystery.

In our language, we call Him *"Ong Troi,"* which loosely translates to something like *"the great man in the sky."* When we're looking for a little luck or a favor, we call on Ong Troi, hoping He's listening. In moments of joy, we let out a cheerful *"Troi oi!"*—kind of like saying *"Oh my Heavens!"*—as if He's right there, sharing in our happiness. But when life takes a tough turn, that shifts to *"Oi Troi oi..."*—our version of *"Oh Lord..."*—a sigh, a plea for comfort, or maybe just a little help.

Standing among nature's grandeur—vast forests, towering mountains, or an endless sky—it's easy to feel small. In those moments, He becomes The Creator, the one responsible for all life and the beauty that surrounds us.

But no matter the name—*Ong Troi, God, The Creator*—we never quite know what He looks like, or even what He truly is. That's part of His mystique. He's the Almighty, always just beyond our grasp.

So we bow our heads, not only out of respect or fear, but to look inward. We examine our own hearts, our swirling thoughts, and the emotions that drift through us like clouds. And maybe, just maybe, we realize that we too are small universes, constantly changing. And when we're honest, quiet, and a little bit vulnerable, we begin to sense Him—not as some distant figure in the sky, but as something that's been within us all along.

So I remind myself: no need to shout His name in desperation or joy. Maybe He's been quietly reigning inside me this whole time.

## 75. FLOWER FRAGRANCE

Every time I stroll down that familiar street, under those towering trees that seem to have been there since time began, past the same old villas with their rusting iron gates and the ancient church, whose yellow walls have been weathered by decades of sun and rain, something curious happens. I catch a whiff of dracontomelum flowers in the air—a scent that seems to drift in from another lifetime.

Of course, there aren't actually any dracontomelum flowers around. Not a one. But my memory has a way of conjuring them up as if they're scattered all over the pavement, tiny yellow and white blossoms, gently falling as if they're being sprinkled over my shoulders. In my mind, they fall on my shirt, in my hair— almost as if they're following me.

I'm suddenly back in those summer days, taking her home after a long afternoon together. We rode our bicycles down that narrow street, enveloped by the whispering trees, their leaves and invisible flowers falling around us like nature's confetti. Back then, everything seemed so simple. Just the two of us, riding through a sea of shadows and sunlight, with the quiet scent of dracontomelum clinging to the air. The flowers weren't just falling—they were following us.

Autumn, though—it's something else entirely. It wraps you up in a soft, golden haze. The sunshine seems gentler, the wind whispers secrets, and the leaves, of course, can't help but join in on the conversation as they drift down lazily from the trees. And just like that, you find yourself lost in a nostalgic daydream, where the past feels as close as the wind brushing your cheek.

It's funny, really. How the scent of flowers that aren't even there can pull you right back into the past—like an old friend who's come to remind you of days that will never quite let go.

## 76. TRAP

Life has its fair share of traps, doesn't it? At first, you're convinced that all these pitfalls are someone else's fault. Maybe it's your competitors playing dirty, or jealous colleagues stirring the pot. Sometimes it feels like you've been blindsided by the entire universe conspiring against you. You think, *"Surely this can't be my doing—this must be bad luck!"*

But as time goes on, you start to see things a little more clearly. You realize that the one setting the traps all along was, well... you. Turns out, those pitfalls? They're just the byproducts of your own mistakes—moments of impatience, foolishness, or a dash of overconfidence. Maybe you rushed things, tried to take shortcuts, or plucked the flower before it was ready to bloom, hoping to speed things along.

I'll be the first to admit it: every trap I've fallen into, I set for myself. Like a hunter who somehow becomes the prey, I've walked right into my own snares more times than I care to count. It's like trying to capture a butterfly and then realizing you've tied yourself in knots instead.

The question is, how do you avoid getting caught in your own traps again? The Buddha says the key is simple: let go of all desires, stop chasing after things, and quit competing. If you can do that, no more traps. You'll be free, floating through life without a care in the world.

But of course, that's easier said than done. So, I tell myself: *"Stop chasing butterflies, stop picking flowers. Just go find yourself."*

It sounds like a long, sorrowful sigh—endlessly repetitive, almost monotonous. But then I comfort myself with this: if, in the midst of your search for yourself, a butterfly happens to land on your shoulder, don't swat it away. And if, by chance, you stumble across a garden of beautiful flowers, resist the urge to pluck them all.

Just be still. And keep going.

## 77. THE ART OF COOKING

I've taken up cooking recently. After a long day at work, I find something almost meditative about slicing, peeling, seasoning, and sampling. It's quiet, it's elegant, and every so often, the drivers lend a hand while I consult my trusty cookbook. Occasionally, my colleagues are the lucky guinea pigs for my experimental dinners in my spacious apartment. I dream of the day when I finally feel satisfied with how the food looks and tastes. But hey, progress is progress!

One day, out of the blue, she called. I've known her for years, though we rarely see each other. She's beautiful, exquisite, the kind of person you drop everything for when she asks if you're free for dinner. Naturally, I didn't hesitate to say yes, and just as naturally, in a moment of inspiration (or temporary insanity), I invited her to my place for dinner. To my surprise—and slight panic—she agreed.

I rushed home early, menu ideas tumbling in my head. I stopped by the wine store to grab both red and white wine, swung by the ice cream shop for some strawberry gelato, and sped home like a man on a culinary mission. I had no more than an hour to prep, but I was determined. Appetizers? Check. Thinly sliced, well-seasoned beef? Check. Soup simmering nicely? Check. Red wine breathing and the whites chilling? Check and check. I set the table, dimmed the lights, and lit some candles—because nothing says "culinary prowess" like candles. A little jazz on the stereo set the mood. The doorbell rang right on time.

She arrived, looking stunning in a long, graceful dress. Naturally, she wanted to see what I was doing in the kitchen, but I suavely steered her toward the sitting room with a magazine and some music. No peeking before the big reveal.

The first course was a colorful salad, paired perfectly with chilled peach-scented white wine. She loved it. So far, so good. Next up: stir-fried mushrooms with five spices, served sizzling hot with red wine. The smoky, earthy flavors lingered, and she couldn't stop with the compliments. "Are you a full-time vegan?" she asked with a mischievous grin. "Not today, dear," I replied.

The main course arrived—fried, red wine-soaked beef. The rich aromas and candlelight combined with the oak scent of the wine barrels, making the meal even more intoxicating. "This is delicious," she said, her eyes sparkling. "I knew there had to be some meat involved." "Consider it my temporary break from veganism,"

263

I joked, taking my time savoring each bite. The beef melted in my mouth as I drizzled some black mushroom sauce over it. Life was good.

As the saxophone softly serenaded us from the speakers, I brought out two bowls of garnished soup. She looked surprised but impressed that there was yet another course. Everything was going down a treat, and she even complimented the soup as a perfect way to conclude the meal.

After the food, I insisted on clearing the table while she relaxed. A moment later, I returned with two cups of strawberry ice cream and frosted glasses of sweet, yellowish wine. We moved to a cozy spot near the record player, where I swapped the jazz for something softer and more intimate—*House of the Lovers.* The mood was just right. She looked at me with admiration, perhaps even a touch of something more.

In the spirit of the evening, I excused myself to change into something more comfortable. A quick rinse, a dab of cologne on the back of my neck, and I was ready. Or so I thought.

Oh, God. I was not ready. When I walked back into the room, she sat there— glasses still on—but wearing nothing else. Her legs crossed, a small glass of wine in hand, her body swayed gently to the music. And we hadn't even made it to dessert yet.

And so, I find myself dreaming of an autumn afternoon like that—where the fish swim peacefully in the aquarium, and maybe, just maybe, the art of cooking leads to something far more unexpected.

## 78. KEEP SILENT

People can be strange creatures, can't they? Sometimes they remind me of chickens. After laying an egg, they squawk and cluck loudly, making a fuss over something as ordinary as breathing. Just one egg? Come on, it's not that special—plenty of chickens know how to lay eggs. It's not exactly a grand achievement.

And let's not even talk about when that egg turns out to be a bad one, a rotten little sin wrapped in a shell. Yet, people are the same way. They love to talk, to explain, to argue endlessly about everything under the sun. And if talking isn't enough, they fill thousands of pages with books on every philosophy, belief, or doctrine imaginable. But, when you step back and look at it, what's really changed?

Materialists or idealists, believers or nonbelievers, progressives or conservatives—it's all just a never-ending loop. History repeats itself. Life spins round in circles. The Creator—or whoever you believe is up there—just keeps turning the wheel.

Sometimes, I think the smartest thing to do is to watch it all in silence. Silently act. If you make a mistake, silently own it. If you don't understand something, learn quietly. And if life throws injustice or pain your way, maybe the best thing to do is to silently endure.

But here's the thing about being silent for too long: it can get lonely. So, every now and then, I sit down and scribble out a few words for myself. It's like I'm clucking on paper! Which, I suppose, makes me just another noisy chicken after all.

Still, I tell myself—this time for real—I'll keep silent from now on. At least... I think I will.